MW01231028

Strength Mindset
The Psychology Of Success

Larry Walser

Legal Notice

All rights reserved.

No part of this book may be reproduced or transmitted in any form or any means, electronic or mechanical, including photocopying, recording, or by any information storage or retrieval system, without permission in writing from the Author and Publisher.

All the product names or logos described within this manual are the trademarks and/or copyrights of their respective owners of the product names or logos and has authorized or approved this publication.

The publication contains the opinions and ideas of its author and is designed to provide useful advice to the reader on the subject matter covered. Any references to any products or services do not constitute or imply an endorsement or recommendation. The Author and Publisher strive to be as accurate and complete as possible in the creation of this book, but do not guarantee that the information or suggestion will affect everyone who reads it.

The Author and Publisher specifically disclaim any responsibility for any liability, losses or damages of any kind as a consequence, directly or indirectly arising from the use and/or application of any content of this publication.

Texts and images available over the Internet may be subject to copyright and other intellectual rights owned by third parties.

Table Of Contents

The Journey Of Self-Discovery 1

The Path Of Self Discovery 3

How To Know The Real You 5

The Value Of Spiritual Self-Discovery 8

Self-Discovery – The Key to a Happier Life 11

We Are Responsible For Our Own Happiness.........................12

Meditating For Self-Discovery 15

Questions You Can Ask Yourself for Self-Discovery................17

What Are The Factors To Self-Discovery? 19

Ways To Discover Yourself 21

10 Questions To Understand Yourself....................................22

There Is More To You Than You Think....................................24

Have You Ever Encountered Yourself? 26

Self-Acceptance Is The Key To Life Transformation................28

Self-Discovery Starts By Loving Yourself 30

Who Are You? 32

Personality Development—How to Reach Your Goals 36

Knowing Your Personality 37

Tips On Personality Development 38

The Little Voices In Your Head 40

How Much Can You Rely On Your Subconscious?...................42

Can You Achieve Success Using Subconscious Mind? 43

How to Take Control of Your Subconscious Mind? 45

Change Your Life by Using Subconscious Mind 47

How to Use a Subconscious Mind to Seek Solutions?............48

How Subconscious Eating Can Affect Us?..............................52

The Conflict Between Good And Bad 53

Self-Reliance Is A Part Of Optimism......................................54

How to Stay Positive When You Are In A Negative Environment?..........55

To Stay Unaffected From Negative Thoughts Of People? 58

Steps to Think Positively 59

Can Positive Thinking Change Your Life? 61

Positive Thinking And Its Effect On Health 64

Self-Love: The Start Of It All 66

How to Fall in Love with Yourself...67
When You Know What Makes You Happy You Discover True Gold..........70
You Are Worth It!...71
Do You Expect Good Things To Happen In Your Life? 74
Love Among People Leads To A Happy Life 76
What Makes You Feel Loved?...77
Accept The Pleasures And Pains Of Life To Make It Beautiful................78
How to Improve Your Mood Swings and Be a Happier Person to Live with
80
Self-Renewal: The Pillar Of Strength...82
It's Not What You Can't Do, But What You Can 86
What Makes You Happy?...90
A Smile Can Change Everything...92
How To Think Happy Thoughts And Learn To Fly.........................94
Is the Perceived Lack of Happiness Robbing You Of Real Happiness?.....97
What Have You Gifted Yourself Today?.......................................98
Your Life Teacher 99
Dealing With Criticism 101
Facing Life Challenges—Accepting Them Or Changing Them 103
If You Could Zoom In On Your Life 105
Achieving Life Balance 109
Experience Your Emotions But Don't Be Led By Them 111
When Things Go Wrong—Are They Failures or Opportunities?...........114

The Law Of Attraction **117**
The Littlest Of Things Sometimes Have The Biggest Of Gifts.............120
The Law Of Attraction And Your Life..121
Learn To Manifest Your Dreams...123
What Are Your Excuses? 124
What You Can Accomplish Within 5 Minutes!...............................126
The Lesson Of The Tortoise 128
Positive Thinking And Determination Helps One To Attain Goals.........130

Embrace The Changes Of Life **134**
How To Create A Healthy Living Habit? 137
Changing Your Self Perception And Feeling Good About Yourself........138
Dealing With A Major Change In Life..140
Anticipating And Preparing For Change And Stressful Situations To
Minimize Distress 142

Here's To A Powerful Manifestation **146**

Inner Strenght Manifesto **147**
    Little Known Way To: Self Assurance!...................................152
    How Positivity Enables You To Achieve More in Life...........................155
    Manifestation At Its' Core...164
    2 Simple Ways To Practice Manifestation 166

The Journey Of Self-Discovery

Have you ever wondered who you really are? What your life purpose is? What are you really meant to do on this Earth, in this lifetime? Do you feel that there is more to you and what you can offer?

If you are still searching for these answers, then you have come to the right place. The journey of self-discovery requires a lot of groundwork and can be daunting at times, as it involves revisiting a lot of your past experiences, choices and emotions.
Therefore, this book will guide you through all the intricate details you require in your journey to unravel your true self. This includes identifying your personality, awakening your spiritual dimension, learning to love yourself as well as embracing the change that comes.

It will no doubt trigger confusion, doubt, and misunderstandings, which will force you to make decisions that will affect your life. However you need to trust the process as it is worth taking and you will turn out to be an entirely different person from where you started off.

There is more to you than you think.

Let go of your past and focus on what is about to come. Give permission to yourself to go through this journey and allow yourself to be vulnerable. When you open up yourself to all the possibilities this journey will bring, you will realize how rewarding it is at the end.

You will discover the most important element of all: YOURSELF

The Path Of Self Discovery

Conducting A Self-Assessment For Self-Discovery

"There is no greater journey than the one that you must take to discover all of the mysteries that lie within you"
-       Michelle Sandlin

To a very large extent, many of us tend to see the wrong in others without taking into account or having a close look on ourselves.
We subconsciously judge others and not ourselves.
Taking a self-assessment is important in realizing and shaping us to becoming the best version of ourselves.
You also need someone who is very honest to help you in your self-assessment.
Usually the person who is able to help you is someone whom you can trust. It can be your significant other or a best friend. Also, there are a number of self-assessment tests that you can take for self-discovery.
Self-assessment involves looking deep into you for an INSIGHT.

Self-assessment does not meansyou are taking some time to reflect upon yourself and get to learn about the person you see every time you look in the mirror.
The first step to a definite self-assessment is to be HONEST about you. Take a good look in the mirror and take the time to study the person you see.

Describe the person you see in the mirror using up to a total of 25adjectives. Consider using both positive and negative adjectives. This exercise is important because you are being honest with yourself. Dig deep. Allow for self-discovery.

The next step is to consider your likes and dislikes. This is important to allow yourself to identify the root of your likes and dislikes.
Write down the activities you love doing.

Which books do you enjoy reading?
What kind of people do you surround yourself with?
What are the activities you enjoy during your free time?

For all the answers that you give, provide an explanation.

Explore the explanations in depth.

The next exercise is to start writing a journal. For a whole week, write down all your emotions, actions and thoughts that you might have.
Write down what you feel most comfortable doing without much effort but is also very rewarding to you.

How To Know The Real You

"Anyone can appear beautiful from afar. The real test of character is how you are to those nearest to you. Good character means that the closer someone comes to you, the more beautiful you are"
-        Yasmin Mogahed

Discovering your real self can be scary sometimes. It demands an understanding of your personal aspirations, emotions and even spiritual values. It also involves knowing how best to fulfill the requirements you want in life. If you come to an understanding of all these aspects of life, then you are on the right path to self-discovery.

What we usually focus on in our lives is to make a living, chasing money and we tend to forget the spiritual part of our lives. We neglect the fact that we need to strike a balance between our physical, emotional and spiritual being.

You need to look inside your soul and search for what it needs. It is important to note that we are not just a vessel but rather we have an inner self comprising of the soul which also yearns for satisfaction.

We need to be connected with ourselves and draw attention or move away from distractions from outside. In most cases, our focus is tuned into meeting our external desires.

There will never be a sense of fulfillment if we keep looking at the outside. In most instances, we are busy with the desire to meet the needs of the physical and this causes one to lose him or herself. Take time to meditate. It will help you realize and know yourselves better.

Another way to help you discover your real self is by improving your relationship with others. It helps you to place your focus less on material gains and more on intangible values like love and honesty.

We will feel more content when we improve our connection with others by making the people around us happy and helping out where we can. This gives us more of a spiritual satisfaction.

The Value Of Spiritual Self-Discovery

"To make the right choices in life, you have to get in touch with your soul. To do this, you need to experience solitude, which most people are afraid of, because in the silence you hear the truth and know the solutions."

-       Deepak Chopra

When people embark on a journey of self-discovery, they tend to focus on the physical and emotional side of their personality.
People rarely take into account the importance of spiritual self-discovery. Take some time to explore the spiritual aspect of ourselves. As a result, we will discover a unique and different aspect to our personality we may not even have realized existed.
We are made up of physical, spiritual, intellectual and emotional dimensions. We experience the universe through the individual and collective lenses of these dimensions.
This is not something entirely new.

We know that humanity has always considered these dimensions. We have been informed through Roman and Greek mythology, Roman astrology and ancient religion how spirituality has played an important role in human development.

We perhaps can relate best with moments like witnessing a sunrise or an amazing act of nature that leaves us in a state of awe and wonder, admitting there are things in our life that are beyond our ability to explain and control. We may consciously or unconsciously acknowledge the desire to discover this power and it is what we can term "spirituality".

When we talk about spiritual well being, we inevitably think of God. Whoever or whatever we conceive "him" to be. Some consider him a supreme being and others consider him as "the man upstairs" a father figure. Some may reject the concept of any sort of being, and find their spirituality elements through earth, or in Mother Nature.

So how do we discover the spiritual side of our personalities?

There are various ways in discovering the spiritual side of our personalities. Some people seek spirituality by embracing formal religion; others discover it through yoga or some other form of meditation that enables them to focus on themselves.

Others go on a journey of self-discovery and call this a

religious experience.

Some have compared this spiritual awakening with a heightened sense of experiencing. As we consciously allow our inner selves to experience life at a deeper level as compared to what seems obvious around us, we begin to relate to things in a different way.

On the other hand, some of us subconsciously or consciously seek help and shelter from a higher being or some of us may refer to as "god" when we find ourselves in a dire position. For many people, this moment is also considered a spiritual awakening. In order to embrace our spiritual side, we need to acknowledge it exists. As we embark on a journey of spiritual self-discovery, we often discover aspects of our personality and our character we have not come across before.

Most of us find that it awakens our inner elements and fills a void in our lives.

Some people perceive having faith or spiritual awareness is like following something blindly without proof, as it is intangible. This is common in the early stages of spiritual awakening, where for many people it is an uncomfortable place to be in. But by the end of the day most of us come to accept there are many things in our lives we accept without proof.

When we discover the spiritual aspect of ourselves, we also discover our place in the universe. We often ask ourselves, "Why am I here" and "Where am I heading."

Whatever we call our spiritual reality; these are two fundamental questions we ask ourselves. Spirituality helps us discover the answers to these questions. Spiritual self-discovery can be a journey that fills us with a sense of personal "completion" and contentment.

Self-Discovery – The Key to a Happier Life

"Success is not the key to happiness. Happiness is the key to success. If you love what you do, you will be successful."

-        Albert Schweitzer

The term "Self-discovery" means identifying yourself and your needs. Self-discovery is very important. If you do not discover yourself, and know exactly what you want from life, you have no idea what you are living for. A step to self-discovery is identifying your needs. Most people are clueless of what they want. To identify your needs, you first need to take a step back and think thoroughly.

Then, when you are in a relaxed state of mind, meditate and focus on your thoughts.

Ask yourself questions like what makes you happy, what makes you sad and so on. Along with the question of what, also ask why it makes you feel certain emotions. Seek a deep and strong reason behind it, not a common or general answer.

When you have identified what makes you happy and sad, you can focus on the things that make you happy and stay away from moments that make you sad.

After you have the answer to all of your questions, write them down on a piece of paper so it will be easier for you to view it whenever you need to.

We Are Responsible For Our Own Happiness

"Don't ever feel bad for making a decision that upsets other people. You are not responsible for their happiness. You are responsible for your happiness"
-       Dr. Isaiah Hankel

We spend a lot of time looking outside of ourselves in search of happiness. We might feel the happiest when we are under the influence of alcohol or other substances. We might need our family or friends around us to feel happy or we might even think that losing weight or becoming fit is the way to achieve happiness.

Whilst these things may contribute to our happiness, our true happiness lies within us and as we find ourselves, accept ourselves and embrace ourselves only then can we find true happiness that is not dependent on external substances or factors.

This can be one of the most liberating thoughts of all self-discoveries.

Once we learn this fundamental lesson, we determine how we react when things are not going the way we plan. Until that moment, our happiness is mostly dependent on other factors rather than ourselves.

Many people perceive happiness as positive emotions. We associate happiness with feelings or emotions that can range from contentment to pure joy. A lot of us tend to put a lot of expectations on external factors to make us feel those positive emotions.

Until we can come to terms that we are our own source of happiness, it's likely our relationships will never live up to our expectations.

They may add to our happiness, but they can never be the source of it.

Henry Miller said, "I have no money, no resources and no hopes, but I am the happiest man alive."

How do we search for our own happiness?

Happiness is, more about the state of mind as a response to it. To seek happiness within, we first need to change our attitude. We must adopt the mindset that happiness exists within, despite external circumstances.

Perspective is the creator of happiness and it may also be the destroyer of it. Training ourselves to remain positive and content is an important life skill.

Once learned, it will help us maintain healthy emotional responses to every situation we face. Alain-Rene Lasage once said, "I am happy and content because I think I am."

Meditating For Self-Discovery

"Meditation means the recognition or the discovery of one's own true self"
-       Sri Chinmoy

Meditating can be a good way of tapping into the subconscious to understand your inner self. It will help you to answer questions you have related to life. Meditation is important in making or deciding the path in which your life should take. However, you should not be discouraged if you do not seem to get the right answers straight away.

Keep on practicing and in the end, you will finally get the answers. When you are meditating, the brain transforms to a theta state. When you are in this state you encounter very minimal interference from the conscious state of the mind. Thus, you successfully make contact with the subconscious state of the mind.

Begin by sitting in a place that is very comfortable and a room that has very minimal disturbance. Consider lighting a few candles so that you have minimal light. Take into account the pace of your breath.

You should practice deep, controlled breathing that comes from the diaphragm. Breathe in and out, where it is advisable for you to use your nose. Pay attention to your breathing.

As you meditate, your mind becomes engrossed in thoughts.

Pay attention as the thoughts come and go. If there's a thought that keeps on coming for long, consider digging deeper into that particular thought.

This is the perfect opportunity for you to search for answers you have been looking for, as your whole being is at ease. Keep in mind that you should not force anything. Do not force the answers but have a receptive and open mind. This will help you discover yourself better.

Questions You Can Ask Yourself for Self-Discovery

"Your vision will become clear only when you look into your heart. Who looks outside, dreams. Who looks inside, awakens"

-       Carl Jung

Even though we are all different in terms of gifts and talents, unfortunately not all of us are well aware of what our gifts are. It is also true that most of us know what our strengths are but they do not know how to maximize them.

We also do not know how to use them both for our own benefit and for the benefits of others. One of the main reasons why people do not maximize on their God given talents is the failure to discover them. Many young people have the problem of identifying who they really are and what they are in this planet.
There are a number of questions that you can ask yourself during self-discovery. These questions are:

- Do you still love doing the activities you were doing as a child?

- If you so happen to write a book, what subject

would you write on?

- What area or aspect in life you feel you can comfortably help people in?
- What does your close associates, friends or even relatives say about you?
- What is your happiest memory?

Search the memory within you and try remembering a certain day that you felt truly happy.

All these questions will lead to the discovery of the REAL you.

At the end of the day, you will have personal satisfaction of the direction or path that your life is ought to take.

You will feel motivated and inspired. You will also be more confident about yourself and you can handle anything that comes your way with ease.

What Are The Factors To Self-Discovery?

"Sacrifice today for tomorrows betterment, you are willing to pay those payments with pain, because pain is just a message when you are fixing something that's insufficient in your life"
-       Greg Plitt

Self-discovery is not a thing that happens by itself. Certain situations and factors lead us to discover ourselves. When we grow up, we have to pass through many challenges and setbacks in our lives. These situations make you who you are.
Listed below are some situations that you may face:

Experience is the most important factor in discovering yourself.
You react in a certain way when faced with certain adversities. This is the time you discover yourself. Even if you think in a certain way, your practical actions in that very situation may be entirely different.

Passionis also a major way to self-discovery.
What you are truly passionate about gives an indication of who you are and what your purpose is.

Environment is another important factor that plays a major role in discovering yourself.

The environment in which you are immersed in shapes who you are. If you are in a positive environment, you tend to discover yourself as a person with a positive outlook, and vice versa.

Thus, the elements of self-discovery are transparent and in one time of your life or the other, you get the opportunity to discover yourself. It is important to discover yourself not only for apparent causes, but also for your inner satisfaction.

Ways To Discover Yourself

"Some steps need to be taken alone. It's the only way to really figure out where you need to be"
-        Mandy Hale

There are millions of people on earth coming from different regions, religions, colors and cultures. In spite of so many differences, one thing is common; all of us have a PURPOSE. Again, the purpose may vary from one individual to the other. Many a times, you may have role models whom you want to follow.

However, many people instead of looking up to their role models for reference, they copy their role models directly. They lose their sense of self and originality. To discover yourself and understand your abilities to achieve, you have to understand the basic fact that you are bound to face obstacles when achieving your target. For instance, when a baby is growing, he first learns to crawl, then he slowly learns to sit, then he learns to stand and then finally, he learns to walk and run. Despite the obstacles he faces, he reaches his aim and successfully walks.

Focus is another important factor related to self-discovery. Many people do not know how to focus on a goal. They simply spend their time doing things that are a waste of time and without proper planning. Therefore, when you strive to reach for the goal place your utmost focus on factors that contributes to the achievement of your goals. You have to exert discipline in your life.

10 Questions To Understand Yourself

"Find something you're passionate about and keep tremendously interested in it"
-       Julia Child

Do you understand yourself? Understanding yourself assists you in making decisions in life. Often the choices we make without understanding ourselves can be wrong decisions that create further problems.

Understanding our strengths and weaknesses helps us guide our paths to experiences that will provide us with the best possible outcomes of our choices.

If you keep a journal these 10 questions may help you in discovering yourself and to get in touch with your inner thoughts and feelings. These questions can help you make choices in your private life, working life and in relationships.

Describe what you believe is truly important in life.

Describe what values you uphold in life that best reflects what you believe in.

Describe your dreams and what you would want to achieve for yourself personally in life.

Who is your mentor or major influence in your life and how do they help you make decisions? Why are they an important influence?

What do you consider your special talents and gifts?

What skills would you like to develop in either your personal or working life in the next 12 months?

What would you regret not doing if you look back in your life in 20 years' time?

What do you consider as your greatest achievement in life?

What do you consider as your greatest failure, sadness or disappointment?

Remember there is no right or wrong answers for any

of these questions. As you answer them honestly and thoughtfully, the answers will provide you with a picture of who you are and a summary of your hopes, aspirations and the things you can learn from your past choices. Turn your answers into life goals and use them to help make decisions that will shape your future.

There Is More To You Than You Think

"If you had not suffered as you have, there would be no depth to you as a human being, no humility, no compassion"
-       Eckhart Tolle

The person you look at in the mirror may not be the person you think he or she is. Most of our self-awareness comes from our perceptions of how we think we appear to others. Just how accurate our thoughts about ourselves are, is usually dependent on our life circumstances and the people and events that have shaped our perceptions.

Some people have achieved a sense of acceptance of whom they are and where they fit into the world. For many people however, the public image they portray to others may not be a true reflection of their inner feelings.

Self-talk convinces many people that there is nothing good in them or their lives. This creates tension and sadness that can manifest itself in destructive ways. It can affect relationships and health if not countered.

How do people develop negative feelings towards themselves?

Often, they are the result of events where someone we love or trust say or do things that make us feel bad about ourselves. It begins to affect the way we think and feel about ourselves and how we appear to others.

Escaping the negative feelings means learning to love the unique person we are. It also means learning to allow others into our lives again without the fear of hurt or rejection. We can do this alone by consciously rejecting the inner voice and countering it with a reminder of all the blessings and successes in our life.

Have You Ever Encountered Yourself?

"You cannot experience yourself as what you are until you've encountered what you are not"
-       Neale Donald Walsch

Actor James Baldwin once said, "I have encountered a lot of people in Europe, I have even encountered myself". It raises the question, have you encountered yourself?

To encounter means to meet by surprise or unexpectedly, amongst other meanings. When was the last time you experienced that type of surprise meeting with yourself?

Have you been in a situation where you found out you liked something you didn't think you would enjoy?

You may try new food, or a new sport. Maybe started a new hobby? When this happens without you orchestrating the situation, you are encountering yourself. Many people stay in their comfort zones, and rarely find themselves in a situation where they are challenged by encountering themselves in an unexpected or surprising way.

As a personal challenge, take time to do something

different today.

Take a walk on the beach or through the forest and use your senses to experience the sights, smells and tastes around you. Walk slowly and keep a journal close.

Allow yourself time to experience things you may usually take for granted and write down the things that you are starting to become aware of.

Write about the way they impact you and if they bring back memories or other significant thoughts, write them down as well.
If you are taking a journey of self-discovery, encountering yourself is the first step to learning about the person you are. Another meaning of encounter relates to conflict and confrontation.

Much of the time we prefer not to confront ourselves and we certainly don't want to know the inner conflict, but for self-discovery to be successful, we must be willing to consider even the inner conflicts we have constantly raging inside us. We must be willing to confront the unjustifiable fears and assumptions we make often with no reason.

Self-Acceptance Is The Key To Life Transformation

"Let go of who you think you are supposed to be and be who you are"

-       Brene Brown

Sometimes in the course of our lives, we find ourselves saying yes to decisions we later regret. As we think of them, we wonder why we keep allowing ourselves to make the same bad decisions. Dwelling on the decisions we make can create a cycle of negative thinking.

The desire to be successful is important to most of us.

We want to be the best husband, or provider for our family, or the best at our job. We want to bake the best cakes or be the best mother or wife. Our self-esteem is often dependent on how others think of us.

Our struggle to achieve great things in our life is often the result of a desire to feel accepted by others as a means of feeling self-accepted.
Even the most confident people have their own insecurities.

For instance, celebrities often resort to face lifts and heavy use of makeup to protect their public image. Being insecure does not indicate failure, but it is part of humanity. When those insecurities begin to drive our decisions and our choices, then we risk making poor decisions and creating inner tension and negative self-talk.

To help develop a strong sense of self-acceptance, it is important to ask ourselves about the intentions we have in making our decisions and what our motivations are behind them.

Sometimes the good decisions we make are not the best decisions. Instead, they reinforce the cycle of trying to find self-acceptance by the acceptance of others. Taking an inventory of our own dreams and strengths is essential to breaking this cycle.

Our value and worth aren't dependent on what others think of us, but more on how we think of ourselves. As we get in touch with our inner-self and embracing who we are, then we are able to make life decisions that contribute to and enhance our self-image. Most importantly, we have come to terms with who we are.

Self-Discovery Starts By Loving Yourself

"Don't forget to fall in love with yourself first"

-      Carrie Bradshaw

Self-discovery is greatly dependent on whether you love yourself. Love for oneself is a great asset that one can have in life. First and foremost, you should ask yourself who you are. To a very large extent, most of us are deeply engrossed on the day-to-day hustles and bustles of life. This entails; making ends meet, running our various businesses and starting new paths for our careers. We are deeply engrossed in this until we forget who we really are. We never stop to discover ourselves. If you do not love yourself, then there's no way you can love somebody else.

Always put yourself first and do not look down upon yourself. Loving yourself has nothing to do with ego; it does not mean looking down upon others or being too proud. There's no way you can love others if you do not love yourself first. Thus, loving yourself opens up your life to unique possibilities as you are comfortable in your own skin and is ready to take on anything that lies ahead.

When Was The Last Time You Experienced Joy?

"If you carry joy in your heart, you can heal any moment"

-      Carlos Santana

Pure joy is that feeling you felt as a child when you were anticipating opening the presents under the Christmas tree as you woke up on Christmas Morning. It is the feeling you felt as a child when you were faced with what seemed to be the most colorful ice cream you had ever seen.

Do you remember feeling excited as you waited for the gates to open at your favorite theme park?

As we grow older, we lose the sense of pure joy that captivates a child's mind. We rarely let ourselves enjoy our activities with the recklessness we did as children In your journal, write down 5 childhood memories that you remember that gave you the feelings of deep joy and excitement, both as you anticipated them, and later as you experienced them.

If for example, eating an ice cream on the beach was a special childhood memory that made you skip with joy and anticipation, then take your family or your friends and enjoy ice cream on the beach with them. If you enjoyed going on a trip in your family caravan during holidays, then hire a caravan, take time to go and explore and relive the adventures with your own family.

As adults, the responsibilities of our lives rob us of simple pleasures that give us joy. No journey of self-discovery is complete without looking at the person we were as a child and comparing the person we are now as an adult. The experiences that shaped our personalities are rooted deep within our childhood moments. Spending time reflecting on them is an excellent way to rediscover our inner self.

Who Are You?

Becoming Who You Desire To Be By Developing Your Personality

"What lies behind us and what lies before us are tiny matters compared to what lies within us"
- Ralph Waldo Emerson

Personality development is a powerful tool that can

really take you to greater heights you never have possibly imagined. Personality development will help you improve on many aspects of your life, which includes; your social health, financial well-being and even emotional health.

Before you get on to personality development, you need to first identify your personality.

What type of personality are you?

What are the strong and weak points in your personality traits?

What are you doing to improve on your weaker traits and what initiatives are you taking to enhance your strong points?

When these questions are honestly answered, you can then move on to the next step, which is the actual personality development. The first thing you need to do for your personality development is to spend some adequate time with yourself. This will help you to be in touch with yourself and you are able to learn more about who you are.

Next, you need to forge the way forward; clearly state the development you want to see within yourself despite your weaknesses and strong points. You need to be realistic and stringent at the same time. Do not be too hard on yourself, as being unrealistic will cause you disappointment. Keep in mind to also not be too soft on yourself, as this will slow down your personality development journey.

Forgive yourself for all the mistakes you have ever committed in life. Trying to do personality development with a grudge and a bitter attitude towards yourself will be useless and will garner no results, as your mind and attitude are hindered by the past. View all your past failures as a stepping-stone to your future success.

Personality development also demands flexibility. You cannot be rigid and expect personality development to work for you. Be open to whatever requirements personality development has. Be flexible and realistic you're your goals as well, because you might need to make some adjustments along the way.
Tune your entire being to personality development, and the journey will be smooth sailing from there. Make it even easier by illustrating what you want to achieve. Picturing or illustrating what you want to achieve helps to keep your progress on track. It is advisable for you to make a daily checklist and set your

goals in milestones. This way, you will obtain your goal in a consistent and realistic manner.

Personality Development—How to Reach Your Goals

"You must be the change you wish to see in the world"

-        Mahatma Gandhi

We come across many people in life, and they are all different in how they behave, react and reason. All of us are made unique by the different personalities we possess. Therefore, personality is the combination of mannerisms and attributes that makes one person distinct and unique from the other. Personality is formed as a result of many factors.

First, there are personality traits that one inherits from parents and relatives. No wonder you find some of your traits and your likes and dislikes similar to those of your parents or relatives. There are some personality traits that we pick up along the way as we grow and live our lives. As we grow older, we pick up habits, values and beliefs that are dependent on our upbringing. However, the traits we pick up as a child tend to make a lasting impression on us as compared the ones we encounter as adults.

If you want to have successful personality development, you need to be honest with yourself on your personality type. Observe the strengths and weaknesses of your personality type. Do your best to focus and build on your strengths.

For instance, if you are talkative and confident, use this to your advantage and let this trait boost your career and ambitions. Also, identify your weaknesses in a very honest and open way.

Work on your weaknesses by making deliberate efforts. For instance, if you struggle with pessimistic thoughts all the time, try and find a way to find the positive in things.

Knowing Your Personality

"Personality is to a man what perfume is to a flower"

-       Charles M. Schwab

There are many ways in identifying your personality type. Nowadays there are various online personality tests made available for you where the results can be accumulated within minutes.
Personality types are classified into different categories, but generally there are four different temperaments – the introverted and the extroverted, the one who thinks and the one who feels, the one who

uses judgment to conclude and the one who uses keenness, and finally, the one who prefers using senses and the one who uses discernment. These different temperaments usually determine how one will react to various situations and the choices one will make. When you have identified your personality type, you get better understanding of yourself.

You are able to maximize your potential and use it to your advantage. For instance, if you are introvert you can channel your talents in ways that suits your personality best.

When you understand your personality type, you will have clarity in your communication with others. You will learn to compliment the other party. For instance, you may be the one who thinks before they act and is very keen as opposed to your friend who uses spontaneity and quick judgment. This creates harmonious relationships.

Tips On Personality Development

"The foundation stones for a balanced success are honesty, character, integrity, faith, love and loyalty"
-      Zig Ziglar

Everyone has traits that make them unique and that

make one David totally different from the other David, though they share the same name. These traits are what sets individuals apart. The environment in which we grow up in and the people we mingle with shapes who we are.

Being honest with yourself is necessary because it will help you to identify your weak and strong points alike so that you are able to use them to your advantage. You can also develop your ability in being a good listener. Listen to others more as opposed to talking to them, and you will be amazed at how much this will help in personality development. When it is time for you to talk, avoid having the "me" attitude. Avoid being narcissistic.

The Little Voices In Your Head

How to Understand The Presence Of A Subconscious
Mind

"It's the repetition of affirmations that leads to belief.
And once that belief becomes a deep conviction, things
begin to happen"
-        Muhammad Ali

Many people assume that they are in full control of
their life. They fail to realize the simple fact that not
everything works according to plan. Not everything is
within our control.

Among these is our subconscious mind.

The subconscious mind has both its advantages and
disadvantages. Most people unknowingly use the
subconscious mind for harmful purposes.

For instance, many people allow their subconscious
mind to take control of them and dwell on negative
thoughts. In extreme cases, this may lead to depression
and worse, suicide.

This is just one simple example. Often these negative thoughts make us feel the need to accept it.By nature, we are prone to look and accept at the negative side of things more than the positive ones.

Let us take a simple example to prove this case. Do you remember the day you lose someone? In most cases, the answer will be yes. What comes after this is the affirmation of your feeling, be it positive or negative. It isthe subconscious mind that plays themajor role in dealing with these feelings. It will either lead you to happier or a sadder one.

If you are constantly expecting something positive about an event, the chances to receive positive outcomes are high as well. No matter the events or past experience you've gone through.

This is similar if your reception towards an in event is negative. Chances are you will receive a negative upturn. Both scenarios happened because your subconscious mind has accepted the fact.

The subconscious mind plays a major role on how we perceive and project ourselves. When you utilize the subconscious mind in a positive way, then it can bring a huge advantage in your life and change your life for the better. Since it involves emotions and feelings, therefore having a positive subconscious mind possesses the power to heal negativity.

How Much Can You Rely On Your Subconscious?

"Follow your instincts. That's where true wisdom manifests itself"

-       Oprah Winfrey

We oftentimes have conversations with ourselveson a daily basis. At times it creates an internal struggle between the different "voices" we often hear when these conversations occur.

These conversations are known as self-talk. Our subconscious is constantly "talking" to us and often answering itself at the same time. The voices we hear and the decisions that arise from our self-talk can potentially help us make important decisions. Buthow much can we rely on our subconscious and our self-talk?

Usually, self-talk is activated when a certain activity or event is about to happen to us. It may be something we see, hear or experience. As we think about the situation at a conscious level; our subconscious also begins to respond.

We may for example, remind ourselves we have an important exam the next day. Our subconscious reminds us that we need to study for it. This may be considered positive self- talk and for many decisions, this type of subconscious activity can be life changing. However on many occasions, it may also produce negative reactions. From previous example, instead of preparing for the exam, it may leave us feeling anxious. It will lead to a hasty decision as we are allowing our subconscious to take control of us.

Perception can be altered by the current state we are in. Identifying whether these self-talk is based on facts or perceptions will help us make a better decision using our subconscious mind.

Can You Achieve Success Using Subconscious Mind?

"It is psychological law that whatever we desire to accomplish we must impress upon the subjective or subconscious mind"

-       Orison Swett Marden

The answer is yes. But the real question is,"How to achieve success using the subconscious mind?".

The mind has the ability to project imagination. Only when one imagines something, one can create the imagination.

You are in control of what you want and it takes place in your conscious mind. The conscious mind will transfer it to the subconscious mind for it to imagine, see, perceive, and feel. This process is what makes a person motivated to achieve their desired success.

Knowing the right method to use your subconscious is the key to a great many benefits. However, it is imperative that you stay positive throughout the process. This is to ensure that your subconscious mind is working for your good intention.

Generally, a human being uses 15%of his subconscious mind correctly. What would happen if human beings used the remaining 95%? Seems farfetched but if it truly happens, there would not have been so much suffering in this world and everyone would have lived in peace.

Mankind would have achieved success at every sphere of his life. Thus, to make a greater utility of your subconscious mind, get to know yourself, learn the proper way, and take control of your amazing mind. However, you must know the appropriate way to turn your negative subconscious mind. Only POSITIVITY can bring success.

How to Take Control of Your Subconscious Mind?

"Your subconscious mind controls all the vital processes of your body. It already knows the answers to your problems and it already knows how to heal you"
-   Dr. Jill Carnahan

Subconscious mind is a highly complex zone of the mind and is difficult to be understood. Those who could are capable to interact with it using their inner voices. It is part of the brain that deals with the emotions and feelings of oneself.

They are part of our sensitive insecurities also, our subconscious minds. That is why it is only possible to take partial control over it by the help of these few steps.

Firstly, you can leave physical reminders. For instance, if you are on a goal to lose weight, write down the dos and don'ts to achieve your goal. You can write them on a piece of paper, journal or even place it on the wall. With it, you can control your subconscious mind with the repeated reminders.

Meditation is the second step to control your subconscious mind. It may be hard to concentrate during the initial days, but with time, you can achieve it. In meditation, you do not visualize anything; you just concentrate on your thoughts, by emptying it. All you have to do is first, relax yourself. Close your eyes and gather all your thoughts to a single point of concentration.

Then release it, while maintaining the relaxed composure. This helps to rationalize your decision-making process.

Visualization is the third step. Once you managed to concentrate on meditation, now is the time to visualize your goals. This step gives you the motivation to achieve your goal. The more you visualize it, the more you are prone to work harder to achieve it.

After all these steps, make promises to someone you trust so that you are holding yourself accountable on your goal.

Inevitably, you will often receive both positive and negative feedbacks from them. If you tackle it using an optimistic attitude, the negative feedback will serve as an urge to deliver the promises.

Change Your Life by Using Subconscious Mind

"Whatever we plant in our subconscious mind and nourish with repetition and emotion will one day become a reality"

- Earl Nightingale

Now that you know the working process of your subconscious mind, it becomes easier for you to inculcate good habits.

For example, if you are addicted to drinking, it is your subconscious mind that has made this habit. Therefore, you must know the mechanism behind it to change your life for the better. That is why research shows that your subconscious mind is heavily linked to your current habit.

What you need to take close attention to is how these habits did grow. The answer is probably these habits did not happen in a day. By constantly repeating some acts or thoughts, you have grown accustomed to the habit.

When you repeat an act or a thought several times, it will reflect on your subconscious mind. In due time, it will accept is as part of your daily routine; habit. That is how your habits grow.

If you want to learn to change and control it for the better, all you need to do is inculcate the same repetitions. But make sure it is made out of positive attitude. Even if you are in a negative environment, you must have the courage to look at things positively. Knowing how to differentiate the good and the bad will help keep you in control of your own habit.

How to Use a Subconscious Mind to Seek Solutions?

"Your subconscious mind does not argue with you. It accepts what your conscious mind decrees. If you say, I can't afford it, your subconscious mind works to make it true. Select a better thought.
Decree, I'll buy it. I accept it in my mind"

Dr. Joseph Murphy

Once you have identified the link between your habit and subconscious, you need to use it to seek solutions. You need to believe in the power of subconscious mind that you can use it to its full potential.

But"How do you use the subconscious mind?" exactly? Here are some strategies that will help you to learn to use the subconscious mind.

Notify the problems you are having to your

subconscious mind. Remember, you need to accept the fact positively in order to seek for the solutions.
Remind the subconscious mind by repeating the problems that you have and stressing on searching for the answers.

Visualize the problem to find the solutions. This is what we call the input step.

Next is the processing step. For this, you have to relax your mind by involving in activities that are not stressful to you, be it listening to music or doing sports. The aim is to avoid stress. The more you can avoid stress, the more easily you can find definite and positive solutions to your problems.

Next is the output stage. After the subconscious mind seeks a solution to the problems, it lets you know by giving you a feeling. The most important thing for you is to understand and process the feeling.
However most of the time, you may not even pay much attention to it because it comes in the form of vague images in your mind. So, the next time you are experiencing this, remember to take a step back and process that feeling. It could lead to the answer you are seeking.

Manipulating Your Subconscious Into Developing Good Habits

"Excellence comes from the practice of developing good habits. It comes from the doing; not the thinking"
Tudie Rose

Once you managed to manipulate your subconscious mind, it is time to develop a better habit out of it. The actions and decisions we make in life happen at a subconscious level. Our subconscious is the "thinking" part of us that drives our perceptions, and often our decision- making processes. It is also known as "instinct" or "gut feeling".

If we do not control it, our perceptions can be clouded by stress and other such factors that can lead to inappropriate reactions.

It is possible to train and manipulate your subconscious mind to develop good habits by focusing on the facts and not being influenced by perceptions. It is also important to remember that when facing with negative self-talk, you may not be able to change the situation you are facing but you can change how you feel about it.

Experts tell us that 90% of the things we worry about will never happen to us. That is why we need to focus on the root cause of our worries instead of mere perceptions;
First, ask yourself about the facts of the situation and as you write them down, try not to reflect on any emotions.

Second, ask yourself if there are alternative causes, rather than the one your subconscious is suggesting. Challenge your perception with evidence from other sources that may falsify your perception.

Put perspective back into the situation by reflecting on the facts and alternative causes.

Challenge the perception you have had and create an alternative perception.

As you learn to challenge the way your subconscious relates to situations, you can manipulate it to start thinking positively. The goal is to challenge your subconscious reasoning before it "thinks" and responds negatively to situations.

How Subconscious Eating Can Affect Us?

"It's the repetition of affirmations that leads to belief. And once that belief becomes a deep conviction, things begin to happen"

- Claude M. Bristol

Despite the many challenges you have to deal with, food and eating habits affects you subconsciously. Subconscious eating is a habit when a person eats instinctively without thinking. For example, if anyone brings you food that you like, you immediately pick up the food and start eating, even if you are not hungry. This practice of subconscious eating generally makes it more difficult for a person to lose weight.

One of the biggest mistakes that people make in their subconscious mind is that they begin to eat more when they workout. If the intake of calories is more than what he burns, then he does not lose any weight, instead he gains even more weight!
Thus, to control the eating habits, you have to play an ACTIVE ROLE. For instance, you are a person with a 220-pound weight and you want your weight to reduce to 121-pound. So, your first step is to visualize yourself as a person of the weight 121-pound.

Only then you will get a positive AFFIRMATION in your subconscious mind to lose the weight and control your food habits. Along with controlling your food habits, you will also need to perform some exercises to reduce the weight. Remember, you are accountable of what you eat. Simply saying that you could not control eating is a mere excuse.

The Conflict Between Good And Bad

Am I A Pessimist Or An Optimist?

"A pessimist sees the difficulty in every opportunity; An optimist sees the opportunity in every difficulty"
-        Sir Winston Churchill

Optimism and pessimism are two contradictory terms. Whenever you want to start a task, you will face it using either a positive or negative perspective. Sometimes certain compulsions leave you to take up a task even if you are not willing to do so.

If that happens, look at the task in a different manner. Think of the benefits it can bring to you. This way you can enjoy the task and start with a positive attitude. A positive attitude leads to a happier state of mind. Whilst negative attitude tend to miss all beautiful things that life has to offer. One of things you might be doing unintentionally is by constantly bemoaning over your failures.

To know whether you are an optimistic or a pessimistic, listen to the voice of your heart. Think of the times when you landed up in a negative situation, and how you reacted during those times. What sort of thoughts came to your mind in those days? How you took charge over the situation?

Self-Reliance Is A Part Of Optimism

"Optimism is the secret of self-reliance. Self-reliance is the secret of a dynamic power. A dynamic power is the secret of an immediate success"
-       Sri Chinmoy

All living and non-living things are independent and they sustain each other. Plants, animals, human beings cannot exist in isolation. They share life together. Although we need others to live, so long as we are not self-reliant, we have not started living properly. It is applicable to individuals as well as to nations. Normally, an individual from the very beginning is taught to be self-reliant. A child is sent to school, then to college to prepare himself to face life. Most of the time, he needs to figure out how to adapt to his new environment on his own.

This is what we call self-reliance. It doesn't mean merely an ability to earn one's living. It implies much more. A self-reliant person is one who thinks without fear and works with devotion. He develops confidence in his abilities, one of life's essential to success.

It is a lesson that should be taught early in life while the young minds are being trained for a vocation. It is education about which can teach the impressionable young apprentice to learn to live and not merely to learn to earn a living.

It helps users in an era, which Mahatma Gandhi had envisaged, where man will not feel degraded if asked to do menial work. On the other hand, he will take pride in being self- sufficient.

How to Stay Positive When You Are In A Negative Environment?

"Staying positive in a negative world will not only better your life but will also change it in more ways than you can ever imagine"
-       Timothy Pina

The essence of achieving a balanced self-reliance is by going through multiple negative environments.

We often end up in a negative environment be it for a short or a longer period of time. The best example to this is unemployment. When this happens, the first impression you will get is negativity. Some people who lose their jobs get a new job within a short span of time, whilst others have to wait.

The frustration and depression reflects on your cover letter and that results in denial of jobs. An employer can easily find out a low self-esteemed person from a high esteemed person.

This influences their decision to hire a new employee.

So, one of the good techniques to stay positive in a negative environment is to jot down the positive things that comes or exists in your life. Do this on a daily basis. For instance, write the names of people who love you, all the possessions that you have acquired these years by sheer hard work. Also, note at least one positive thing that you have done in the day. This feeling is important to stay positive in a negative environment.

In days when pessimism is likely to set into your mind, engage yourself more in outdoor activities that interest you. You might be a little hesitant at first to go out, but once you go out and engage yourself in the outdoor activities you will start thinking positively. Engaging yourself in your interests is not a waste of time rather it is useful.

To Stay Unaffected From Negative Thoughts Of People?

"Don't let negative and toxic people rent space in your head. Raise the rent and kick them out!"
-        Robert Tew

Sometimes, even if you believe that you can get through all the negativity surrounding you, you will see that there is no end to it.

Pessimists are at every corner of the world, always looking forward to ruin your day. They derive satisfaction from indulging an optimistic person into negative thoughts. Therefore, it is always advisable to stay unaffected by the words of these pessimists. Here are few ways to help you out.

Often negative–minded people will come to you first when you are in a turbid situation. They come and make all the possible negative comments to put the fear into you. Do not take their words into your head. Instead, politely respond to them to ensure that you do not lose your decision-making capabilities. Taking things personally is a major mistake.

Another way to deal with negative people is to do them an equal amount of good for all the negative things they do for you.

Confronting them will shake their confidence and make them rethink about their attitude. Demonstrating their attitude and letting them know how mean they are may make them change their attitude a little. This will show the real optimism in you.

Steps to Think Positively

"Life is 10% of what happens to me and 90% of how I react to it"

-      John C. Maxwell

In life, we will never be able to avoid challenges. It is part and parcel of life. There will always be ups and downs and whenever we face challenges or difficulties, you would have heard people dispensing advice to stay positive and have an optimistic mindset.

However, it can be a challenge to constantly stay positive when things don't work out they way you want them to. But further negligence will be harmful for your health. So here are 3 effective ways to stay positive.

First, at the beginning of each morning when you wake up, immerse your mind in positive materials. You could read positive quotes or listen to motivational talks and the whole idea is to ignite your day right with positive energy.

In fact, going through the quotes in this book helps too! If reading is not your cup of tea then listen to speeches and talks.

Second is to speak positively. Words carry power and energy especially those that you say to yourself because the kind of language you use influences the perception you create towards an event or occurrence. For example, when you drive out to work and you get stuck in a traffic jam, you've got a choice.

Do you curse and swear at your luck, or acknowledge that there is nothing that can be done so might as well make the best use of the situation? Consider the two outcomes, one involves swearing, the other may involve singing in the car and through the jam.

Third, accept total responsibility. This is by far the most effective but difficult for people to accept. Accepting total responsibility is very powerful. This means that whatever your life is today, you are responsible for it. Whether you are rich or poor, healthy or not, it is the culmination of all the decisions that you made and did not make.

Accepting total responsibility creates personal power and because you always have a choice, you can change the course of your life if you so wish to! You just have to decide by exercising your responsibility on your life!

Can Positive Thinking Change Your Life?

"Change your thinking. Change your life! Your thoughts create your reality. Practice positive thinking. Act the way you want to be, and soon you will be the way you act"
-       Les Brown

These days, people seem to be focused on making a living instead of making a life. There's a huge difference. One focuses on the lack of while the other focuses on using what is already there. When there is too much focus on chasing money instead of balancing with experiencing life, there is a tendency to get depressed due to the pressures of life.

Sure everyone will face pressures in life and what I believe to be the best way to manage it is to practice positive thinking. Positive thinking is a process of consciously thinking and expecting positive and good results in all aspects of life, be it finances, health, relationships and so on. The thoughts and focus is on the positive outcome and through this, you will feel all the good vibes. This positive energy will have the ability to move you forward even in difficult times.

But what if you just can't help it and you perceive yourself as a pessimist? Well you can change your outlook and thought process if you so decide to but it will not be a sudden change or it happens within a day. It all depends on your time, patience and willingness.

You will find challenges if you decide to change and more often than not, the challenge will come in the form of your inner voice.

In your pursuit of adopting a positive mindset, your inner voice may become your biggest sabotage if not managed properly. Therefore, first you have to learn to identify your inner voice and bring it to awareness.

Know that not all which you say to yourself is true.

For example if you are thinking of buying something which requires a bit of a financial stretch for you, do not think or respond that the item is too expensive instead ask a better question. Ask, "How Can I Afford This?".

What happens is your mind will seek for answers to make it happen and you will be amazed with the results.

Positive Thinking And Its Effect On Health

"A strong positive mental attitude will create more miracles than any wonder drug"
-       Patricia Neal

We all know that feeling sad can lead to depression if it's not resolved. Research has shown, that people who are positive thinkers tend to have fewer colds and live longer and enjoy being in a state of good health.
The reason for this overall improved state of health is not hard to understand. There is a direct connection between our emotions and our physical body.

This connection has been known for a long time, though not completely understood. People grow old physically but when they maintain a positive outlook in life, they remain young and confident on the inside and their energy levels remain high.

The feeling of being optimism about life in general helps us make better choices in other areas of our life. Those who feel relaxed and confident tend to eat better food, exercise more, and spend more time with family and friends. These activities contribute to an improvement of health and wellbeing.

It just simply means reducing the stress in our lives and remains positive despite all we may be facing. Emotional well-being is one of the most important gifts we can give to ourselves. Doing regular emotional checkups and ensuring we do something to aid our emotional well-being is essential to maintaining a healthy life.

Self-Love: The Start Of It All

Self-Discovery Starts By Loving Yourself
"Don't forget to fall in love with yourself first"
-     Carrie Bradshaw

Self-discovery is greatly dependent on whether you love yourself. Love for oneself is a great asset that one can have in life. First and foremost, you should ask yourself who you are. To a very large extent, most of us are deeply engrossed on the day-to-day hustles and bustles of life. This entails; making ends meet, running our various businesses and starting new paths for our careers. We are deeply engrossed in this until we forget who we really are. We never stop to discover ourselves.

If you do not love yourself, then there's no way you can love somebody else. Always put yourself first and do not look down upon yourself. Loving yourself has nothing to do with ego; it does not mean looking down upon others or being too proud. There's no way you can love others if you do not love yourself first. Thus, loving yourself opens up your life to unique possibilities as you are comfortable in your own skin and is ready to take on anything that lies ahead.

How to Fall in Love with Yourself

"Perhaps, we should love ourselves so fiercely, that
when others see us they know exactly how it should be
done"
-       Rudy Francisco

Do you love yourself?

Most people would probably evade the question, but it
is an important and valid question which if we could all
answer yes to, would change the way we feel about
ourselves and give us self-confidence to achieve the
dreams and desires we have for our lives.
It is also about accepting that we have our own special
place in this world. Feeling unloved and unworthy is a
very lonely feeling. If you cannot find anything to love
about yourself, you are probably struggling with self-
love.

Learning to love you is possible. To love yourself you
must challenge the negative feelings inside that center
our thoughts. We must acknowledge that our self-
worth and self- acceptance are about the person we are,
the person we are comfortable being around when
everyone else has left and when we are alone. We must
realize by the end of the day, we are all we have.
Take the time to sit and write all the things there is to

love about yourself. Be honest with yourself. Do not let toxic thoughts hinder the process. Try to do these five simple things every day and you will find yourself thinking differently:

Write down positive qualities you possess and read them aloud to yourself often.

Learn to self-care and do something every day that you enjoy. You deserve it!

Look in the mirror and learn to love the person looking back at you and tell him or her every day that they are loved and why.

Fill your life with people who love you and tell you often what a special person you are. Accept their words and their love without questioning it.

When you have positive affirmations about yourself, you automatically begin to love yourself and you are ready to take up any challenges ahead

You Are Reborn Each Day...

"The world is new to us every morning – this is God's gift; and every man should believe he is reborn each day"

-       Baal Shem Tov

With each morning that you wake up, it is akin to you being reborn. You are given a new chance at life again, to pursue and make life for what it is to you.

Think about it. With each breath you take, you are alive and that means you have the choice to completely change the direction of your life and everyone has this choice. It is by no means that you are forced to do something. You always have a choice. Every second of your life is an opportunity, a choice.

So this means that each day, you have 86400 opportunities; to be reborn and change your life direction. There is power in making a true decision in that moment.

To assist you in making this decision, I want to share with you the Countdown method.

This method is simply a proven way to assist you to make laser focused decisions and exercise your decision making muscle.

How Does This Work?

Simple. The next time you feel as if you can't decide or you don't know what you want. Countdown from 4..., 3...,2...,1...and decide. It's that simple. Follow you gut feel and decide. This is effective because it eliminates over thinking and paralysis through analysis.

When You Know What Makes You Happy You Discover
True Gold

"A beautiful heart can bring things into your life that all
the money in the world couldn't obtain"
-       DauVoire

Do you know what makes you happy?

If you do then you have discovered true gold. We are
not talking of the momentary flashes of happiness that
come when we eat a favorite desert or drive a beautiful
car. These will provide temporary happiness but once
the dessert is eaten or the car is returned to its owner,
the potential is there for the problems that robbed you
of your happiness to return.

The happiness being discussed here is the happiness
that you can take refuge in, that keeps you at peace
with yourself and your world, no matter what is going
on around you.

Some people find a sense of happiness in their
relationship with God. For some, happiness is found in
pursuing a new hobby or learning a new sport. Many
define their happiness through their roles in life.

However, are these things really the source of true happiness?

Self-acceptance is the key to help us deal with the everyday trials of life. We may express self-acceptance in our relationship with God or with others. However, unless we accept ourselves first, nothing will truly satisfy us or make us happy for very long. Psychologists have long promoted the idea that the greatest love affair we can have is the one we have with ourselves.

Even if we are hit hard by what life may throw at us, it cannot really harm us. We can experience that level of true happiness when we learn to love ourselves and see ourselves as the true gold we are. We can find refuge in self-acceptance, knowing that we are not defined by our experiences, but rather we can define our experiences by our reactions to them.

You Are Worth It!

"Self-worth comes from one thing- thinking that you are worthy"

-        Dr. Wayne Dyer

Do you feel you are not good enough?

Everything you do feels like it eventually amounts to

nothing so you don't even try?

You find yourself spinning in a downwards spiral because you feel like you don't measure up?
For those who feel this way, this might be their "reality" or truth. Research has shown that the feeling of unworthiness is one of the common contributing factors of weight gain and emotional eating disorders. We all have room to grow and develop and the most liberating truth of all is that each of us is unique and beautiful. There is no one quite like you on this earth and there never will be.

Once we accept this, we can then focus on ways to improve ourselves. Without appreciating this perspective, it feels as if we are constantly striving to find self-acceptance externally instead of willingly and wholeheartedly accepting ourselves for who we are. This creates an unhealthy dependency on external validation. A person who only feels happy when people praise him or her will never genuinely feel happy because external

praises will die down and is not long lasting. People can't be praising us 24 hours, 7 days a week.
An old African proverb reminds us if there are no enemies within, then no external enemies can cause us

harm or hurt. This means that if we are at peace with ourselves then whatever events or occurrences that are perceived to be bad and negative will not affect us unless we allow it to.

So I want you to challenge those thoughts.

Starting tomorrow - Choose one action to do for you yourself. It could be as simple as taking that trip to the beach which you have always wanted to or buying that shirt which makes you look good. Give yourself a gift just because. It doesn't need to be fancy if you don't want it to but you MUST feel the genuine feeling of giving yourself a gift and rewarding yourself.

Thank yourself for bring you this far in life regardless of the outcome because you know what? You're still alive!
Most people have to battle self sabotage and rarely say anything nice about themselves but you're not most people and that's why you've picked up this book.
You're looking to improve yourself so take this activity seriously for yourself.
You are worth it!

Do You Expect Good Things To Happen In Your Life?

"When you expect good things, your mind is open to seeing the opportunities. When you expect bad things, your mind is closed. You don't even see opportunities right in front of you"

-       Matt McWilliams

Research shows if we expect good things to happen in our life they often do. Feeling positive isn't some magic formula that guarantees success, but there is a direct linkage between our feelings of positive expectations and the release of endorphins in our brain that act as natural painkillers. This in turn helps to deal with stress and difficulties by thinking with a clearer mind in finding solutions to problems.

The reverse happens when we have low or negative expectations of outcomes. If we think negatively about things, the release of the same endorphins is inhibited. We tend to feel more depressed and it becomes difficult to think or even consider positive outcomes in a difficult situation. When this cycle of negative thinking continues, it has the potential to become a habit and a strong habit requires a big enough pain in order to break the habit.

The expectations of those around us also influence the expectations of ourselves. This is true for both negative and positive expectations. Teachers and parents who have positive expectations on a student's ability to produce a specific quality of work will encourage students to do better.

A motivated person with high expectations of themselves and belief in what they want to achieve, will seek ways to achieve their goals and dreams and this in turn produces endorphins that help to maintain focus even when there are challenges in front of them. Each small success increases the positive expectations and outcomes.

An unmotivated person is weighed down by self-doubt, risks focusing on negative outcomes and expectations and often develops tunnel vision and self sabotage.
If you are in a state of low self-expectation and negative thinking, surround yourself with positive people who are committed in helping you re-focus and raise the belief in yourself and in what you want to achieve in your life.

The most important question to ask yourself here is do

you expect good things to happen in your life?

Love Among People Leads To A Happy Life

"People grow when they are loved well. If you want to help others heal, love them without an agenda"
-      Mike McHargue

In the universe, the one highest feeling is love. When you operate from the intention of love, all things feel possible. All things feel bright. The opposite of love is not hate but fear. Fear is a limiting feeling; it makes us operate from a mindset of "not enough", of scarcity.

Love on the other hand, brings courage, determination, understanding and all other positive emotions.
When love is present among people regardless of race or background, there is understanding, peace and progress. The opposite is acts of violence out of fear. Fear of the unknown, of being threatened and of unrealistic fear.

If love alone could be adopted as the guiding principle of individual's lives, there would be no quarrels and divorces between married. There would be no friction between parents and children, no bitterness between friends, and no exploitation of man-by-man.

What Makes You Feel Loved?

"As we express our gratitude, we must never forget that the highest appreciation is not to utter words, but to live by them"
-       John F. Kennedy

What are the things others do for you that make you feel loved?

Do you like to have people give you special gifts, or to send you cards and messages assuring you that you are loved and appreciated? Maybe you are the type of person who appreciates a hug as a way of feeling loved, or really enjoy spending time with your spouse or best friend.

The way we give love to others is often indicative of the way we want to be loved ourselves. Most couples enjoy expressing their love to each other. However, many of us have yet to learn a golden lesson.

Often what makes us feel loved is different to the way others give and receive it. Learning what makes our spouse or children feel loved is the key to experiencing deep passionate relationships.
We all enjoy being told we are loved, but for some

people, the spoken word is not enough. Telling your spouse or child you love them but never following up with the things that make them feel loved can create feelings of confusion and concern in even the best of relationships.

Learning to recognize the things that make us feel loved and then identifying what the significant people in our lives need to feel loved is a beautiful self-growth adventure that will improve our relationship. It takes little time and effort to learn how to do this, yet as we learn and use this simple technique, our relationships can be transformed.

Accept The Pleasures And Pains Of Life To Make It Beautiful

"The secret of success is learning how to use pain and pleasure instead of having pain and pleasure use you. If you do that, you're in control of your life. If you don't, life controls you"
-       Tony Robbins

In this busy world today, people are always in a hurry. Due to this hurry, they are always competing with each other and it in the process, it is definite that one wins and the other loses.

When a man achieves something or wins, he or she gets a feeling of a natural high, whereas when he or she loses, he or she feels down. It is a known fact that in this earth when the sun rises in one part of this hemisphere, the other part is in darkness. The same fact applies to life too, there are both sorrows and pleasures in life. Thus, life is like a boat sailing at sea that does not always flow smoothly. If a person does not realize the pain or suffering of life, then he cannot understand the joy of life.

Some people have the notion that life is only about sufferings. These type of people forget the happiness they've enjoyed during the past times. They get shortsighted that they forget to feel the basic law that happiness will re-visit them once again in the future. The basic law of life is happiness and sorrow co-exists with one another. Without one, the other is useless. Thorns of life serve as a fence to protect the flowers of delight and sunlight.
E
ven, Shelley – the great English poet said, "Our sweetest songs are those that tell of saddest thought." In fact, comedy and tragedy make the warp and woof of life. All the patterns of experience are woven with these contrasting threads. Smiles are sighs and spice to life

which otherwise becomes dull and monotonous. Even in scriptures, it is written to take joys and sufferings placidly without any hesitation. He is exhorted not to be overly happy when success visits him and not to fear when pains and misery affects him. The greatest of men on earth, all have suffered both the pleasures and pains.

How to Improve Your Mood Swings and Be a Happier Person to Live with

"I've learned over the years that people are human and have mood swings, regardless of how talented they are. Today, I'm looking
at life from a realistic point of view instead of the way I would want things to be"

-      Otis Williams

Do you find yourself getting upset with yourself for being bad tempered and moody around your family and friends?

Our emotions often create mood swings in us and learning about our hormones and body responses to stress can be useful. However, often it's not our mood swings but rather its factors within our control that have created the moodiness in us and thankfully this is something that we can learn to control.

Learning to identify them and reverse their effects on our psyche can help us become happier and more controlled in our interactions with others at work and at home.

If we don't get enough sleep, we will become moody. Every adult should ideally have between 6 and 8 hours of sleep each night. Most people need at least 7 hours sleep, yet usually we find the time we have available for sleeping is getting lesser as our lives become busier. Increasing the amount of sleep will help us control our mood swings.

Check your diet. Ensure you are eating a balanced diet that includes plenty of vegetables and fruit, grains and nuts, protein sources and carbohydrates. Cortisol, a steroid hormone is produced when we are thirsty or hungry and this hormone reduces the immune system and increases our feeling of stress. It is easily reduced by eating and drinking and accounts for the feeling of well-being many obese emotional eaters feel when they eat.

Engage in a whole brain activity, such as a sport or other fitness activity to improve your feeling of well-being and reduce your stress levels. These activities have been shown to improve emotions, logic and ability to learn. This explains why women attending a gym regularly describe feelings of euphoria at the end of their work out session.

Too much television and computer time can affect your moods. The addictive nature of television and computers can create tension and anxiety when they need to be turned off or is interrupted, regardless if how important the reason.

You yourself can be the cause of your mood swings. Author Jeff Conley once said"we must take a checkup from the neck up" When we are feeling stressed or upset, we should try to minimize the damage by tuning up ourselves and our families and seeking to create a harmonious home for our families.

Self-Renewal: The Pillar Of Strength

Time Out For Self-Renewal And Self-Development

"The greatest weapon against stress is our ability to choose one thought over another"
-       William James

Time out is a period of solitude where the focus is on

self-development and self-reflection. It can be an extremely beneficial activity. When was the last time you treat yourself to a nice night alone, or a short trip from home?

Sadly, most people don't take time out. Why? They either have family to take care of; crazy working hours or they just don't have the time to do it. Granting yourself a time out is an act of self-renewal. This is the time for you to refresh your mind and focus on things you want to achieve.

Let's take a look at the benefits of making this a priority at least once a year;

Taking extended time out gives you the chance to take a step back and decide how to move forward in your life. When you are in the middle of life and all its responsibilities, it's easier to focus on survival and not on achievement. Take the time out each year to achieve some life goals.

Time out is not a selfish activity, but a time to be critical and honest about yourself and your life. The focus is to improve your relationships and to help your family and friends. It gives you the opportunity to evaluate what you are doing currently and how you can improve it.

Taking a few hours or a few days out of your busy schedule is not running away from your responsibilities. Rather, it is an opportunity to develop a new enthusiasm so you can keep "running towards them".

Most people are keen to take the time out but struggle with how to achieve it. Here are some suggestions: Discuss with your partner.

Decide on taking the time out together or individually. If children are involved, try to get the help of grandparents, siblings or friends.

If you are doing it with a partner, try to schedule alone time during your retreat as well as time together. Once you have scheduled a time out, it is essential to plan on how to make the most from it. Preparing for the journey is as important as being there. Here are some suggested ways to prepare for your time out experience:

Choose a location that will help you to relax. Whether or not it is close to home, the key is to relax and refresh.

Don't bring anything that will act as a distraction. If you take your cell phone with you, try to borrow one that does not allow you to be tempted to check email or spend time on the Internet.

You can take a personal tape recorder or a journal to enable you to record your reflections and goals as you create them.

If religion is important to you, take a religious book or self-help manual if you would like to use them as part of your meditation.

When you arrive at your time out location and begin the process of self-reflection, here are some guidelines to help you focus:

Evaluate what caused you to feel sad and happy as you review your life. These will help you to focus on things that need addressing in your life.

Celebrate the things you have achieved, and goals you have accomplished.

Create action plans for those things you feel sad or dissatisfied with.

It's Not What You Can't Do, But What You Can

"I've learned it's important not to limit yourself. You can do whatever you really love to do, no matter what it is"

- Ryan Gosling

Do you find yourself focusing on the things you can't do and lamenting the fact you can't do them? Do you wish that you could do some things you enjoy doing better than you can do them? Most of us do have these thoughts and handle them in different ways. Some just continue to do them and some approach them differently. So, instead of focusing on what you can't do, focus on the things you can do and work on doing them even better.

When we focus on perfecting what we are already doing well, we begin to feel good about ourselves. Every day we hear our self-talk telling us conflicting stories. Our friends may praise us for something we have done or the new clothes we are wearing, but we find it impossible to accept that praise graciously and without making an excuse for it. Our negative self-talk will often speak louder than the words of our friends. Focusing on the things we know we are good at, will help us boost our self-esteem.

Take time this week to enjoy and appreciate the things you are good at, particularly the ones you believe you can do well. Take advice from your partner or your friends if you are not sure where your strengths lie. Enjoy focusing your time and energy on helping the good become the best and then enjoy your achievements. Allow yourself to enjoy comments and

appreciation of your work.
It Is Your Life! Embrace It

"You only live once, but if you do it right, once is enough"

-       Mae West

Think about your life today. Is it where you want it to be? Think in terms of your relationships, habits, finances, spiritual well-being and even work. All these things impact on the person you want to see yourself as.
Remember, if you don't take control of your life, someone or something else will take control of it for you. As children we were often asked the question "What do you want to be when you grow up?" Teenagers dream about their perfect relationship and young adults plan their next overseas holidays. As maturing adults, we need to recapture our desire and dreams.
Why not take a life inventory and write them down in every area of your life that is important to you? Search the internet or your local library for opportunities to develop new skills or new knowledge in those areas you want to grow in. Ask yourself these questions:
What are my goals and dreams?

How do my goals and dreams fit into the circumstances of my life at this moment?

What areas do I need training in to achieve my goals?

Who will be the best source of advice to take control of areas that are out of control now?

Where can I find resources to help me achieve my goals and if I can't find any myself?

Where can I go to find the information I need in order to start my progress towards achieving them?

What things in my life need to change so I have time to achieve my goals?

What attitudes in my life need to change so I have the intention to achieve my goals?

With whom can I share these goals with so that I have someone to be my cheerleader as I embrace my goals? Each of these questions help you to prepare insights into yourself, your ambitions and goals to create a practical way to work towards achieving them and embracing the l ife you want for yourself and your family.

What Makes You Happy?

"Life is better when you do what makes you happy regardless of what others think. It's your life, not theirs"

-       Sonya Parker

Ask yourself, what makes you happy? We often spend a lot of our day "in the pursuit of happiness," but do we ever find it or are we on a fruitless road to nowhere when we seek to find it?

Some people try to find money in wealth, others in possessions. Some seek their happiness in their husband or wife or their children. Every day, women around the world go in search of happiness by indulging in "retail therapy." For others, that decadent box of chocolates represents happiness. Men might be smiling at those images, yet how many men have to have their night out with the boys or their weekend golf game.

We will try our best to achieve happiness even if it is going to be momentarily. People will let us down, chocolate will make us fat and possessions just never seem enough. We won't find happiness if we look for it externally. We will never be content unless we first find contentment within ourselves and the world we live in each day.

Here are some thoughts that will help you discover how to be content and achieve happiness:

Don't spend money to find happiness: You will never be happy if you think money can buy happiness, or that happiness lies in possessions. It just leads to discontentment.

Don't worry about the future: Your happiness is available to you today. Many people live in hopes that tomorrow they will be happy. Expect happiness to be yours today!

Find your happiness in believing: Life without belief is a life without hope.

Look at others who are in a worse situation than you and be thankful for what you have: Contentment and gratitude are the easiest paths to inner happiness.

You need to want to be happy: Someone wisely said once "Who does not want to be happy"

Help Others: Their pleasure and appreciation will

increase your own happiness!

"Don't worry, be happy..." True happiness lies in those four small words. Being happy is a choice, not a pursuit!

A Smile Can Change Everything

"Something as simple as a smile can change everything"

-    Stephen Welton

When we are worrying about something, it usually shows on our face. We often think we are looking and acting normal, but stress and worry usually manifests itself in some way.

Smiling is often the last thing we feel like doing, particularly in the darkest of times. Yet, when we learn to smile in spite of our problems, we open a door to a new kind of energy that can sometimes bring relief from the pain we are carrying.

Someone once said, "Smiling is a social obligation." How many times has your day been brightened by the smile of a total stranger? In that instance, when you instinctively smile back at them you find yourself feeling a little optimistic.

When we smile, our brain releases a hormone that makes us feel good. This immediately lifts our spirit and makes us feel more optimistic. Smiling soon becomes contagious. As we smile at people, often people will smile back at us.

Most people when they feel stressed choose to stay at home because they say, "they don't feel like socializing." Instead, go out with family and friends and don't isolate yourself.

Likewise, when you are not with your friends, find a hilarious book to read or watch something humorous on television. Laughter produces a positive chemical response in our brain.

Counter negative feelings by focusing on things that will create uplifting thoughts rather than negative ones. Surround yourself with happy people and fun situations. These will help you to think positively about your situations as their own optimism rubs off on you.

How To Think Happy Thoughts And Learn To Fly

"The moment you doubt whether you can fly, you cease forever to be able to do it"

-       Peter Pan

Peter Pan was asked by his friend Wendy on how she can fly like him. He replied that to fly, all she had to do was to think happy thoughts. Although this was a children's story and a fictional character, the moral of the story remains true. Thinking happy thoughts may not help us fly, but we can be as happy as we choose to be.

Many people allow their life circumstances to control them. Their sense of happiness rises and falls depending on what is happening in their life. This shouldn't be the case. We can focus on our happiness every day. Happiness is a state of mind, not a reaction to the events in our life.

There are some ways you can help yourself to feel real happiness and you can practice these every day:
Help other people.

As long as your focus is always on yourself, you are aware of things that are not as good as they could be in your life.

Find something to be thankful for every day.
Look around your world every day and find at least one thing to be thankful about each day. Write it down in a journal and review your journal regularly to help you remember the good things in your life.

Surround yourself with good friends.
Happiness is contagious as you should have known by now. As you surround yourself with happy people who are positive, their happiness will affect you and your happiness will affect them.

Head down memory lane regularly.
Your life is full of happy memories. Write down why those things made you happy and laugh with someone who remembers them often.

Nurture those you love.
"How much time do you invest into improving your marriage, or developing your parenting skills?"
Research shows that the happiest people are those with the strongest relationships with their significant others.

Look after your health.
Enjoy yourself running around with the children, doing

Zumba at the gym or playing golf with your mates. Looking after your health fills you with energy and when you add laughter to the fun you are the winner!

Try something new you have always wanted to do. Set yourself a challenge to do something new every week no matter how much you feel you can't do it. Have a go and enjoy the experience. You may find yourself surprised by the results.

Don't expect too much.
Keep your expectations on yourself and others at a reasonable level. If you set the standard too high, you are setting yourself for disappointment. Accept and appreciate the things that people do for you.

Happiness is in our reach if we focus on achieving it. Appreciate the good things in our life and the gift of love that is given to us by our significant others.

They are the things that remain constant when other things in our life are not going as well. They help us keep the difficult moments we will inevitably face in perspective and give us hope when things around us may seem hopeless.

Is the Perceived Lack of Happiness Robbing You Of Real Happiness?

"Surrender to what is. Let go of what was. Have faith in what will be"

- Sonia Ricotti

Do you often feel life has left you short, that somehow you have been robbed of the right to be happy and content? Maybe you have financial or relationship issues in your life or you are facing chronic health problems.

There is no one on this earth, no matter how rich, famous or successful who does not suffer moments where they feel that life has served them a difficult basket of trials to deal with.

Other people wear smiles because they have learned to deal with their pain and problems and focus on the good and not the bad in their life.

However, finding the blessings in life and focusing on it rather than the negative is the key that opens the door to contentment. Every person is a unique human being and is the product of their past experiences. The potential for conflict is always there when people interact with each other.

As we focus on the good in the other person and the benefits of our relationship with them, it helps us put a different perspective on the difficult area of appreciation.

Sometimes differences may be irreconcilable, but often-true happiness is not the same as perceived happiness and constantly comparing our relationships or our life with others circumstances will only serve to drag us down. As we learn this essential life lesson, we can learn to explore and find happiness where we least expect it.

What Have You Gifted Yourself Today?

"How could you expect people to treat you well, when you don't treat yourself right?"
-        RafaaKhiari

Depending on which culture you were brought up in, you may be raised to be a good giver or a good receiver. Generally speaking, if you came from an Asian background like Japan, you were brought up to give and think about the community and group first before your individual needs. There is neither good nor bad in it unless you are a good giver but not a good receiver. People who only give but not receive will not fully understand the joys of receiving and will be unbalanced.

So how do you know if you are not a good receiver?

Well the question to ask yourself is, what gifts have you given to yourself recently? Have you treated yourself to something that you really want?

Do you downplay compliments that come your way or do you agree and receive them gracefully?

When you are not receiving properly, it's hard for more joy and miracles to happen. The universe is constantly giving and wants to give but you must be open to receive.

Start today by fully accepting a compliment and believe in it. Start by treating yourself to something that you've always wanted and be happy about it. When you start receiving more and more you will realize that you are in a much better position to give more because you can only give what you have. So fill yourself up first!

Your Life Teacher

How To Deal With Behaviors That Irritate You In Others

"Don't let the behavior of others destroy your inner peace"

-       Dalai Lama

Each of us has developed a set of values that determine how we think and feel about life,
including the right and wrong behaviors. When we see other's doing things that are outside our acceptable behavior parameters, we usually react in a negative way.
Learning to accept the 'what is wrong to us may not be wrong to others', is an important part of personal development. We may not agree with their choices, but we respect and allow people to be themselves. They have values and ideas that may differ from yours.

We act the way we do mostly because it is often originated in our childhood experiences. Like, we have been told to eat with our mouth close. To us, it is a manner that we consider important to ourselves and our families to try and achieve. So when we interact with people who have not been taught of such rules, it is inevitable for us to be frustrated with them.
Often our values and behaviors become the measure for everyone else's behavior.

We cannot always control our reactions to the behaviors of others, but we can learn to control the way we see and respond to them.

Dealing With Criticism

"Take criticism seriously, but not personally. If there is truth or merit in the criticism, try to learn from it. Otherwise, let it roll right off you"
-       Hillary Clinton

"If you keep your head when all about you are losing theirs and blaming it on you" is a line from Rudyard Kipling's famous poem "If." There are probably many of us who can identify with the words and understand the frustration of being misunderstood or unfairly judged.

Almost every day either we or someone we love experience this frustration. How we respond is according to the poem, the measure of our manhood and womanhood. Learning how to respond to criticism and to deal with the negative things people say to us is a step of maturity.

Criticism is an attack on our self-esteem and our defensive attitude would be to protect our self from a painful experience. We sometimes apologize for our behavior or those of others. We even look for ways to blame others for the situation.

So what are some of the positive ways we can respond to criticism?

Look at the incident as an opportunity for learning and self-growth and not as an attack on your self-esteem.

Much of the anger that eventuates from criticism has the risk of becoming a grudge. So always make an effort to forgive the person. Actively seek to work with them to negotiate a solution you are both satisfied with.

Try to take a step back before you respond. Thank them for their words and tell them you will consider and discuss it with them on another occasion. This approach enables both of you to calm and rationalize your actions further.

Think about the criticism; ask yourself if it is justified. If it is, then seek ways to prevent the situation from recurring and, if it is not, take steps to refute it calmly and preferably with evidence.

Don't dwell on the criticism but move on. Your value is not determined by one piece of criticism!

Facing Life Challenges—Accepting Them Or Changing Them

"Life is meant to be a challenge, because challenges make you grow"

-       Manny Pacquiao

Do you sometimes feel that your life is going in the wrong direction and it is out of control? When we face these types of situations, we have two choices. We can either accept that there are things in our lives we cannot change, and there are things in life we can. When there are things in our life we can change, then we must not wait for things to change, but we must work at changing them. Many of us know that certain things in our life must change. However, we procrastinate on making that change to improve it. If we leave it be, it can control our life. Francis of Assisi once asked for the "courage to change the things that can be changed and to accept the things that can't be changed and the ability to tell the difference." The prayer of Francis asked for the ability to tell the difference between the things we can change and the things we can't change. This is the first step towards finding the solution to a bad condition. We need to ask if the situation can be changed. If it is possible, what are the practical steps we need to bring about the changes?

Having determined the answer to that question, we need to put steps into place to help us make the change.

If we decide the change can't be made, we need to try to see the situation in the bigger picture. We need to accept the problem is here to stay and our goals must be on how to relegate the problem and value the life we have apart from the problem.

If You Could Zoom In On Your Life

"The Purpose of life is a life of purpose"

- Robert Byrne

If you could take a photo of your life today and then zoom in on something special or important, which part of your life would you choose? Would it be something that is causing you distress or the opposite? If your still picture was a movie, what title would you give it? Would you like the experience to continue or do you wish it had never happened? If you could relive this part of your life again, would you? If not, why wouldn't you?

Imagining our life as a movie or a photograph is a good way of examining our life further. When we give important life experiences a name, we can focus on the important events in our life and especially on the ones that continue to influence us today.

Have you ever noticed when you take a wide angled shot of a scene you see a lot of picture but very little detail?
Even if you zoom in on one part of the picture that interests you, you miss out on the bigger picture.

We often look at life in this way. We look at the big picture and forget the details that bring beauty and interest to our lives. We are at risk of losing a range of perspective if we only look at life from a single point.

We need perspectives to understand our life experiences and its purpose.

Revisit your photographed memory again. How different does the picture look close up and how does it look at a distance? If the picture is distressing, close up, try to zoom back and

look at the picture from a distance to give you a bigger perspective. Does it change the picture at all?
So you see, if we focus on our life from a distance, we forget to appreciate the individual and smaller things that make life unique.

The Importance Of Conflict Resolution That Validates The Other Person's Perspective

"Whenever you're in conflict with someone, there is one factor that can make the difference between damaging your relationship and deepening it. That factor is attitude"

- William James

Most people approach differences of opinions whilst other people attempting to defend their point of view. Our intention may be to defend our personal position, but most people view our defensive stance as attacking their viewpoint.

It can create confrontation and easily leads to interpersonal issues with the other person. This approach to conflict resolution creates many avoidable arguments in the work place and home.

So how can we present our point of view without creating this reaction in people? The key is to learn to see the situation from the other's point of view and address it from within their viewpoint as well as from our own. We can still express our thoughts and feelings about a situation using this approach, but it usually produces a very different outcome.

This technique is an excellent way to approach all communication, whether with family, friends, work colleagues or strangers. We learn to express our thoughts, concerns and ideas and even disagree with others, but acknowledge verbally and through our body language, that the other person has the right to their opinions and thoughts about the issue causing the disagreement.

This approach maintains a relationship between two people that acknowledges that no one position is more valid than another's views, perspectives or thoughts. This does not mean that both ideas are equally valid, but conveys the understanding that the other person has a right to the thoughts or opinions about the situation causing the disagreement. This approach values the relationship and validates the person, whilst not necessarily validating the problem or the suggested solution.

There is an old saying that states, "you will never know another person until you first walk in their shoes." Trying to approach and diffuse a situation from their perspective enables us to walk in their shoes in the situation. It changes the "I want" statements, which presents the issue from our perspective to the "I know you feel this way and I can understand why you do, but may I present another idea or show you why that idea is not the best one?"

As we learn and apply this technique in our lives, it becomes obvious we have gained insight into an extremely important life lesson that validates and maintains relationships, even if we don't agree with the other person. It helps us to approach potential conflict situations in a non-confrontational way that promotes discussion and resolution.

Achieving Life Balance

"There is no such thing as work-life balance- it is all life.
The balance has to be within you"

-        Sadhguru

Most of us have things in our lives we want to do, as

well as those things we have to do. Perhaps you want to go to the gym more often, or you want to read more books this year. Like most of us, do you find yourself wishing you had more time for those things?

Whilst time management is important to achieving these goals, some other steps must precede it. As you define these steps, preferably using a journal to keep track of what you discover about yourself, they will help you to achieve work and life balance that will enable you to do those things you want to do and achieve at this point in your life.

List Your Goals

All of us have goals that change regularly and that reflect other things going on in our life at the time. List your goals and prioritize them from important to least important. Include not only the goals you have to achieve, but also the personal goals you want to achieve.

List Your Daily Schedule

Although we want more time in the day, all of us have 24 hours. We use some of these hours for sleep and some of these for work and recreation purposes. List down your daily schedule and include the things you must do because they are a commitment. This may include work commitments or school sport commitments with the children.

Prioritize Your Personal Goals with Equal Priority as Work Related Goals

Don't minimize the time available to do the things you want to do, particularly if they are contributing to your life goals or well being. Include family time and other essential life activities that require your time and attention.

Keep to the schedule unless it is an emergency

Most people who create a daily schedule, keep to it for a while, but not long enough for it to become a habit. Habits take around 3 weeks to form, so if you want your new approach to work and lifestyle to be maintained, you must protect it at all costs. If you want to achieve your own personal goals, you must protect them at all costs. Eventually, the changes you implement will become second nature, but until then, you need to stay in control of your time management.

Experience Your Emotions But Don't Be Led By Them

"Do not be afraid to experience your emotions; they are the path to your soul. Emotions erupt to remind us we are alive, that we are human. And to let us know we are

growing. Trust yourself enough to feel what you feel"
-       IyanlaVanzant

Jackie M Johnston once asked her audience. "Have you learned to tell the difference

between "experiencing your feelings and being led by them"? The answer to this question is very personal and is a question each of us must ask ourselves. We cannot begin to act and think positively until we have learned to experience and deal with our feelings, without being pulled down by them. Most people are led by their "gut instincts" when making decisions. How people feel about something often dictates whether they do it or not, or enjoy doing it or not. They may even choose not to do something because of how they feel about it.

The issue with this type of reaction is that, it is deeply rooted in the emotions and not in logic, although logic and feelings may lead us to the same conclusion. This is what is meant by "experiencing your feelings". Have you learned to tell the difference between "experiencing your feelings and being led by them?".

Experiencing your feelings enables you to rise above your feelings then logically decide what action to take.

This is particularly important if you have an argument with a spouse or child. It is very easy to be led by feelings as the argument becomes more heated. A wise spouse or parent, on recognizing and understanding the increased feelings of frustration and anger welling up inside them, will suggest time out to give each person time and space to think and respond logically rather than emotionally.

Learning to differentiate between acting on our feelings and understanding how they can help or hinder our actions and reactions is essential to achieving positive thinking. Negative feelings can hold us hostage to ourselves and difficult to achieve our goals in our life. We don't feel happy or fulfilled with what we have, so we strive for more. We feel depressed so we isolate ourselves from others or we overeat. We feel angry so we take it out through our attitudes to our children or our spouse.

As we learn to channel our negative thoughts and feelings into more positive decision-
making, we are able to use them to help us choose behaviors but we don't let them dictate our actions without first challenging them by thinking through alternative options that can positively affect our lives and the choices we make.

When Things Go Wrong—Are They Failures or
Opportunities?

"Failure is simply the opportunity to begin again, this
time more intelligently"
-       Henry Ford

Many people try new ideas and when it doesn't go well
for them, they give up and feel like failures. Others,
after trying new ideas and failing, refuse to give up and
continue to try and as a result, they end up successful.

Why do some people choose to make the most of the
experience no matter what the result may be and
others rate it a failure if things don't go well? The
answer is an optimistic attitude to every experience in
life. Successes are achievements enjoyed today and
failures are learning tools for future experiences. There
are no failures; they are simply steps towards future
successes.

Learning to laugh at our mistakes and to dream big
dreams are two very important characteristics that
optimists develop that enable them to look at
something that some may call as a failure as a learning
opportunity.

When we take ourselves too seriously, we are more likely to think of our failures as permanent and they often attack our sense of self-worth.
When we can focus on our other successes and see this as a setback that we can laugh at and continue to dream of success next time we maintain our optimism. So how do we deal with failure so we can see it as a learning tool for the future?

Challenge what you think of success and failure. It's our perception of them that makes us see failure as negative and success as positive. Failure is simply part of the journey to success, the ultimate destination.

When you feel like a failure because of a poor result or outcome, set goals for yourself immediately, deciding how to continue your journey to success. The old, but familiar saying of "climb back on your horse immediately after you fall off" is based on this concept.

Look at a failure from the perspective of the big picture, not the small picture. You may have not achieved the outcome you wanted, but you did achieve. Make a list of all the things you learned and gained from the experience and celebrate those things. They are achievements, it is not one complete failure, but many small achievements and they deserve to be celebrated.

Failure is about opportunity and embracing failure as opportunity helps to eliminate failure from your vocabulary helping you to stay optimistic and find success in everything you do.

The Law Of Attraction

Always See The Good In Things

"Give yourself permission to say no without feeling
guilty, mean, or selfish... Be at peace with your
decisions"
-       Stephanie Lahart

When was the last time you watched a bee as it busily
went from flower to flower collecting the nectar and
pollen that would become the life saving energy source
for the larvae back at the hive? While some bees are
happy to collect pollen from many different plants and
flowers, others specialize in only collecting from certain
species. The honey produced in the hives of these
specialist bees is highly sought after for its unique
qualities and flavors.
When making life choices we can be like the specialist
honeybee, taking the good things offered to us in life
and rejecting the rest that will potentially harm us or
our quality of life. Learning to say no is a powerful tool
that many of us rarely, if ever, use.

Learning to reject or say no to what will hurt or harm us in the long term is the key to reducing the amount of stress we carry each day and to feeling better about ourselves, as well as the choices we make.

As we learn to reject the things that will harm us, we are more inclined to accept the things that will help us. How can you tell the difference between what to accept and what to reject to help you stay focused and happy? You need to identify the causes of your distress. Growing through stress is sometimes not an entirely bad thing and sometimes we do need to move outside of our comfort zone to achieve progress in our lives. The key to knowing what will produce good stress and what will produce negative stress is to have a life plan and only accepting those things that contribute to it.

The Half-Full Glass And Positive People

"Doesn't matter if the glass is half-empty or half-full. All that matters is that you are the one pouring the water"

-       Mark Cuban

Do you know a person who is always happy and positive about themselves and life in general? They never seem to have a problem and they are able to deal with things in life with composure and grace. Do you wish you were more like them and you are able to deal with your life circumstances like they do?

These people have a way of seeing life as being the "half full glass" where even if things are going downhill, they find something positive to focus on. This way of viewing life is natural for some people, but for the majority of us, it is a learned response. It results from making an intention to look at the positive and to not to dwell on the negative.

Unfortunately, it sounds so easy but in reality, difficult to execute. How do people learn to focus on the half-full glass and not the half-empty one and remain positive? It's not easy to be thankful when faced with difficult circumstances. However, practicing gratitude helps us deal with the most difficult experiences we may face in our lives. It is the key to optimism and seeing the good in everything.

Half glass full thinking seeks to clarify a situation before complaining about it. It asks whether a complaint will make the situation better or worse and if it will help to resolve the issue. In most cases, the answer to both these questions is, no.

A clear perspective on the situation can help us resolve

a situation. Maintaining an attitude of gratitude helps us maintain a positive perspective on most things that happen in our life. It helps to keep the glass half-full even in the most difficult circumstances.

The Littlest Of Things Sometimes Have The Biggest Of Gifts

"Heavy hearts, like heavy clouds in the sky, are best relieved by the letting of a little water"
-       Christopher Morley

We are always surrounded by beauty. The challenge is whether we allow ourselves to see it because life can be very distracting especially if you live a fast paced lifestyle. If ever you feel stuck, take a pause to be inspired by your surroundings.
Some of the greatest paintings of all times were inspired by nature. "Irises" by Van Gogh, painted in 1889 was inspired by simple flowers. The thing is that these inspirations are free and ready for you to access it whenever you so choose. The key is to be present.
Here is an effective way to be more present and it is the art of doing things slowly, deliberately and more consciously.
Prepare a bowl of mixed nuts in front of you. You can do this at any time of the day.

When you are ready, slowly reach out to select any nut and bring it close to you. Feel free to feel and analyze the texture. You can do whatever you want with it. The goal is to fully understand and focus your awareness to that single nut.

Next, put the nut slowly into your mouth but don't chew it yet. Taste the nut in your mouth first before you chew and when you chew, do it slowly. Focus to find the taste of the nut instead of the act of chewing.

Allocate at least 10 to 15 minutes for this exercise. You may feel the need to rush through something as simple as eating nuts but refrain from doing so. Rushing through it defeats the purpose of this presence exercise.

What you will find at the end of this exercise is the discovery of joy in something as simple as eating a single nut. You would be surprised at how much taste and aroma can come from something simple when we bring our focus and awareness to the current act. You may feel that this is something trivial but hey don't take my word for it. Try it out and see for yourself. Don't miss out on the simple joys.

The Law Of Attraction And Your Life

"Your whole life is a manifestation of the thoughts that go on in your head"
- 	Lisa Nichols

The law of attraction in our lives has become "the thing". Everyone wants to apply this law in their everyday activity. This is because all of us have dreams and we would want these dreams to come true someday.
Most of us want a very successful life with plenty of achievements and happiness. We all want to have our desires to come true. Therefore, the law of attraction helps us to tune our minds and feelings to draw the lifestyle that we want.

Here are steps to active the Law of Attraction

The first thing to do is to describe the type of life that you want and be able to see it in your mind's eye. When you want something, you should ask from the cosmos and you should also have a picture of what it is. Recognition of your dreams and requirements first begin with forming a mental image of whatever you want. Visualization is very important because you are able to involve both your conscious and your subconscious mind. When you do this visualization process, it is important that you feel as if you already have it.

The next part is to think positively. If you are negative, the Law of Attraction cannot be activated. If you want to achieve the success that you want, then you must be positive. Always think that there are different ways to achieve a goal. Positively affirming yourself is the most important thing.

You should also always be thankful and be willing to share the things that you have. This way, you will be able to attract more. Always look at what you have and not what you do not have.

The last thing that you need to do is take massive action!

Learn To Manifest Your Dreams

Achieving Your Dreams

"If you can dream it, you can do it"

-       Walt Disney

Our thought process plays a big role in our successes. Researchers have said that the concept "We are what we say we are" is a statement that we often want to admit. Our state of mind drives our actions. We achieve in life when we can visualize our success. It is at this moment our resolve, determination and confidence kicks in.

Don't let yourself spend time focusing on what you can't do, but rather on what you are doing and what you can continue to work on towards your goals and dreams. No one ever achieved anything without dreaming and determining to put the dream into action and succeeding.

It cannot be emphasized enough that your thoughts are your worst critic, but it is also your best ally. Your thoughts are partially responsible for your actions and behaviors and most people trust their personal perceptions on things that happen in their lives. Channeling thoughts to bring out the best is essential to reaching personal goals.
Surround yourself with people who will support your endeavors and ask them to help you counter your negativity. Nip it in the bud before it has time to blossom into something that causes you to lose your focus. Think of yourself achieving your dreams and you are half way to success.

What Are Your Excuses?

"If you really want to do something, you'll find a way. If you don't, you'll find an excuse"
-        Jim Rohn

All of us have something we really want to do but keep finding excuses not to. Maybe you want to start on a walking routine each day but there is always a house chore to do that "must come first."

Maybe you plan to take up golf, but there is always one more report to write for work. We are so good at making excuses about why some things are more important than other things, but truth is, life balance means that prioritizing time for the things we want to do is as important as doing the things we know we must do.

We all know how important a diary is and the importance of scheduling our time and planning to achieve the things we need to accomplish. In theory, we would love to execute each and every activity planned for the day as written in our diary, yet still we make excuses at the end of the day when we fail to check out everything from the list.

When you did not manage to complete all activities as targeted within the day, write down the last five things you intended to do but didn't accomplish and state the reasons why you didn't accomplish them.

Be honest with yourself about the excuses you made to

justify why you didn't do them. Maybe you felt too tired, or maybe you were fearful of walking that track alone. Maybe you decided to cook a nice dinner for your family instead of going to the movies. Remember, excuses don't have to be negative. Excuses are really choices we make. Sometimes we make choices that are valid, other times; our choices are a reflection of other things going on in our lives. Therefore, writing down our excuses, is really about writing down our choices.

Why did we choose not to do something? Did we simply choose to do something else? Perhaps we were able to modify a choice to make it more achievable. Once we know why we make the choices we do, we are in a better position to change our actions, attitudes or behaviors if necessary to make better choices. Our choices are the essential key to how well we prioritize looking after our mental, physical and inner health.

What You Can Accomplish Within 5 Minutes!

"Peace of mind for five minutes, that's what I crave"

-       Alanis Morissette

Does your life seem out of control? Do you always feel

like you are running from one activity to another? If yes, let me introduce you to the power of 5 minutes. Do not underestimate the importance of 5 minutes! No matter how hectic our days are, we all have 5 minutes to spare in our day and it can do so much to change our perspective on how we go through our daily lives. What can be accomplished in 5 minutes and how does it help our journey to self-discovery?

Take 5 minutes each day to clear out some clutter in your life. Maybe a work area, a pantry or a garage. Allow yourself to enjoy the moment when you have completed it! Organizing helps us think more clearly and set our focus. Research shows that people with a tidy work area achieve more productivity than those with a cluttered area.

Take 5 minutes to go for a walk and find something beautiful in your world you haven't seen before. It will open up a way to count the other blessings in your life that often stay hidden from view as we are often too busy to enjoy them.

Take 5 minutes to do some exercise and marvel at how fit you feel today than you did yesterday. If you don't have time to exercise for long periods during the day, 6 sets of 5-minute mini workouts add up to a 30-minute routine every day.

Take 5 minutes to pray, meditate or have some periods in your day, where you reflect on yourself and your spiritual health and well-being.

Take 5 minutes to fix a proper meal for your family and not find yourself too busy so you buy take away every night. Your body needs good nutrition.

Go to bed 5 minutes earlier each night so you improve on your sleep cycle gradually. You need at least 7 to 9 hours of sleep to help maintain your focus and alertness.

The Lesson Of The Tortoise

"It does not matter how slowly you go as long as you do not stop"

-        Confucius

Do you remember the story of the Tortoise and the Hare? They set out to have a race and in the beginning, it was the hare that have easily bounded ahead of the tortoise and almost made it to the finish line. But this is not before the tortoise managed to go very far at all.

Yet, the hare was just a little too self-assured and he decided to sleep before crossing the finishing line. He slept for so long and so soundly, that the tortoise eventually crossed the finish line while he was still sleeping. Against all the odds, the tortoise had won the race.

We are often told that "slow and steady wins the race" and there is truth in that. What is interesting about this story is that both the tortoise and the hare were using their natural talents. They used them to the best of their ability. From the point of view of Personal Development, maybe we should take a closer look and see what happened in this story.

The tortoise, while not fast entered the race with the best of intentions. He knew he probably would not win, but that didn't stop him from participating. No doubt, he went full speed and put his heart in the endeavor. He didn't just set out on a walk in the park on a sunny day. He fully utilized his abilities and in the end, it paid off and he won. No one was more surprised than him to find that he crossed the finish line first.

The hare likewise used all his abilities, and should have won the race, but he didn't. He had yet to learn the value of not having too much faith in his own abilities. He became so self- assured that he became arrogant. That caused his downfall.

When we compare ourselves to the tortoise and the hare we can learn some important life lessons that may help us in our endeavors. The tortoise did what he did best, to the best of his ability. He did not let circumstances overwhelm him, but instead he did what was asked of him and he eventually found success. The hare likewise did his best, but he let the circumstances get the better of him and they did overwhelm him and he rested on his laurels rather than continuing to the finish line and he found failure.

It is worth asking if in our endeavors we find our successes by having the attitude of the tortoise, or are more like the hare, and rely on our reputation and this explains our failure to succeed.

Positive Thinking And Determination Helps One To Attain Goals

"Believe in yourself and all that you are. Know that there is something inside you that is greater than any obstacle"
-       Christian D. Larson

It is not just enough to think positively. You also need to act on your beliefs and thinking. This is where will power comes into play. Decisions and the persistence and patience to pursue a goal relentlessly take will power.

It is a great force in the world. Couple this with tenacity and purpose and you are unstoppable. However, if you waver at the first signs of difficulty, you will never achieve your goal as will power is weak.

Take for example, Nelson Mandela fought for the freedom of South Africa and during his fight, he was imprisoned for 27 years. If it was not for the sheer conviction in his belief and willpower on what he was fighting for, was it possible to last for even a year in prison?

Definitely not.

The thing is that willpower is present in all of us, we just have to exercise it to be strong and harness it. Here are 3 steps to increase and harness your willpower.

First Be Aware Of Your Limitations. List down an area which you like to improve on. At most times, an easy area is health and fitness because it is something which you can do freely and get results when you are consistent. In that category, pick an activity which you would like to focus on getting results in. It could be running, weight lifting or rope skipping. The next time you do such an activity, measure your results.

Push Yourself. After measuring your results on an average of 3 times, the next step is to push yourself. Stretch your limitations until you can go no more and go even further. So let's say you've run 5 miles in 90 minutes consistently for the last 3 times, you stretch yourself by aiming for a shorter finish time. Set a goal, prepare for it and execute.

Celebrate! With each completion of your attempt to stretch yourself, celebrate your result even if it did not meet your goal. It may sound as if it does not deserve it but here's what happens. With each celebration you are associating good vibes and feelings to the act of exercising your willpower and stretching your limitations. And guess what happens when you truly reach your target? You celebrate even bigger!

Do this and you'll start to condition yourself to break your limitations and it becomes an enjoyable activity.

Embrace The Changes Of Life

Why Is Changing a Habit So Difficult?

"You'll never change your life until you change something you do daily. The secret of your success is found in your daily routine"
-       John C. Maxwell

Changing habits is like getting out of your comfort zone and this is a very difficult task to undertake no matter how desperate we are. Most people have habits they would like to modify be it physically, mentally, spiritually, or even emotionally.
Habits become deeply ingrained in our minds. Changing it can really turn out to be a daunting task. To be able to make the change, you must focus on the behavior you want to achieve and not the one you want to eliminate.

Ever wonder why it is easy for some people to change while others just can't? You see, when you have that burning desire on your subconscious level, you are more likely to get it without having to endure much pain. The only way to execute change it is to look back at the issues that may have been affecting your perception in terms of your behavior. This will help both your conscious and subconscious work in harmony to produce a great achievement.

Write and rewrite your perceptions that limit you from being a better version of you. Once you have the behavior that needs change, then we can look at how to initiate and maintain a change;

Pre-contemplation: Here the person has yet to uncover their problem and they may try to avoid the subject

Contemplation: A person is aware of their problem but unsure if they want to make a change. They realize they should have done things differently but don't.

Preparation: A person is ready to make the changes, they are not completely willing to, but they are ready to change. Mostly this stage is entered when change is unbearable.

Action: Now in this stage the person gets ready to make changes.

Maintenance: The affected person has to learn to maintain the changes and be cautious not to relapse or else they will have to go through the stages all over again.

Changing Habits That Are Deeply Ingrained In The Subconscious

"The secret to permanently breaking any bad habit is to love something greater than the habit"
-       Bryant McGill

But have you experienced that even after all the contemplation, the habit that you tried to change is blocked by something deep inside you? You have sought help from counselors, psychologists and spent money to every self-help seminars, only to find yourself at the same position you were in before?
This is because our habits monopolize our lives. That is why it is important to be aware of our bad habits and replace them with constructive habits. If you have yet to achieve your goal, then you ought to really examine your approaches to life.

I suggest you prepare a list of how you perceive things around you or your attitude toward life. Of course, you will have those that do not serve you well and you don't have to beat yourself down because of it.
All you have to do is eliminate them completely and replace them with their opposite ones. Whatever your

perception is, your subconscious takes it in and it will become a self-fulfilling prophecy.

So instead of saying disheartening to yourself or the situation you are in, think of the past achievements or think of how much you can achieve and how easy life is if only you apply the right skills. You may not believe it initially, but I advise you to keep doing it to the point of faking it until you make it no matter how long it takes. This exercise requires full time dedication. Otherwise you will easily give up. Keep the positive attributes coming in until it steers you directly into your dreams.

How To Create A Healthy Living Habit?

"We are what we repeatedly eat. Healthy eating, then, is not an act, but a habit"
-      Felicity Luckey

We often think of habits as negative things. Even though we would prefer not to do them, we still do them unconsciously. It is useful however to consider that habits can be both good and bad, and that good habits are beneficial to us, and just as removing bad habits are important.

Habits are formed in three weeks. Changing our life style, or eating different foods, or choosing to go on a daily walk will become second nature to us if we can maintain the CONSISTENCY. With discipline, maintaining the new habit will be effortless.

The key to developing these healthy habits is to move them from the conscious level to the subconscious level. They should become something you do without thinking. For example, you want to walk for half an hour before work each morning. Thus, it is crucial that you walk each day at the same time you've set. Nothing should prevent that walk from occurring.

After 3 weeks, if you do not do the walk in the morning, you will feel as if you have missed something out of your morning routine.

In forming new habits, it is normal to have a weak moment when your resolve weakens. When this happens, it is important to focus on putting the weak moments "behind you" and start the process again with no hesitation. With patience, the consistency will pay off and you will succeed in forming a new healthy life habit!

Changing Your Self Perception And Feeling Good About Yourself

"Don't be pushed around by the fears in your mind. Be led by the dreams in your heart"

-       Roy T. Bennett

Now, how do you feel about yourself today? Are you
thinking that if you could just lose weight you would
feel happy and perfect? Are you wishing you had
enough money to buy the hot new car that will make
you the envy of your mates?

For many of us, our physical images and possessions
help define what we think of ourselves. Unfortunately,
that is a shoddy way of thinking and that seems like we
are living in the future rather than in the present.
When this attitude of "life will get better when
something happens" affects the way we live our life, we
need to challenge those thoughts. If we don't love
ourselves now, we potentially can keep on looking to
what the future might do to help us to improve
ourselves. We need to embrace the person we are now
and see that the better resources are already inside us.

Unless we want to lose weight for ourselves, our weight
loss attempts probably won't be successful. We can
hinder our own development and achievements if we
try to live in the future. By embracing the opportunities
we have today, we are more likely to achieve our goals
and ambitions in the future.

Our self-worth is not dependent on what we do. Unless we learn to enjoy and appreciate the person we are, we are more likely to bash our achievements.

The danger of this approach is that if we fail in our expectations, it undermines the way we think about ourselves. Our self-esteem remains weak and we usually feel less incentive to keep trying new things. If we base our self-worth on accepting ourselves as we are today, every achievement can be celebrated.

Dealing With A Major Change In Life

"Change is the law of life. And those who look only to the past or present are certain to miss the future"
-       John F. Kennedy

Ask yourself; ever had anything major happened in your life? When these things happen, especially when we feel betrayed or let down by people we love, it's easy to feel that we can never trust people again. The effect of one or two negative things in our life can cause us to spiral down on a path of seemingly no return. We may even lose confidence in our own ability to make good decisions.

Being stuck in the past and letting the past manipulate and dictate the future is a major reason many people feel that their life does not progress. That is why ACKNOWLEDGING it is the first stage of healing and progression towards a new tomorrow.Remember, no matter what changes that is heading your way, always remember your self-worth.

If you recognize that some incident in the past is affecting your present actions, it is wise to seek professional help or the leader of your religious group if you have the faith in God.
There are also some other things you can do to help yourself.

The past is the past and nothing that can be said or done will change what has happened. Having acknowledged that maybe the past is causing us to have negative thoughts, we can change them to positive ones by focusing on a new beginning.

Challenge yourself to see yourself not as you were in the past, but as you want to be in the future. Write down how you want life to look like ten years from now and write it as if it was a reality. Read it regularly and see how it changes. You'll be surprised at the result.

Anticipating And Preparing For Change And Stressful Situations To Minimize Distress

"To be prepared is half the victory"

- Miguel de Cervantes

All of us face change in our life. Sometimes we look forward to it and enjoy the preparations that are involved in making it happen. On other occasions, change can be very distressing.

Usually occurring without warning and we are usually unprepared for it. We can feel quite disorientated when change is unexpected and it can produce physical reactions we may feel we have little control over. Facing unplanned change with a prepared mind helps to re-orientate life even when it seems to be out of our control. If we accept that change is inevitable, we see the sense in thinking about and preparing to deal with it well ahead when it actually happens. It also helps us to reflect on how we will deal with our responses when faced with stress and change.

Taking the time to plan and prepare for change is not inviting fate, but facing reality. People who work in

occupations that involve dealing with sudden
unexpected emergencies are in a

state of readiness at all times. They learn to anticipate all possible scenarios by learning how to deal with them before they occur. They learn how to prevent or minimize the damage.

We gain valuable insight into how to prepare for change by learning how to apply their approaches to potential change and stressful situations. We prepare for change, or potential stresses in three ways:

Firstly, the higher the risk of something happening, the more we should anticipate it likely to happen. People living in areas where there is a considerable risk of a natural disaster occurring, prepare for its inevitably, by preparing their surroundings each year and psychologically being ready for it.

Contrary to what people may think, being psychologically prepared for change is possible. Although it is impossible to know what it will be like as a parent. For example, we can prepare ourselves by reading and identifying possible areas of concern we may personally face in our new parenting role.

Thirdly, we can also learn to manage our responses and thoughts in times of minor changes and challenges. As we do this, we are providing ourselves with invaluable training. Learning how to deal with the many minor challenges and changes we face daily, will help us to develop the skills to deal with the unexpected major ones.

Here's To A Powerful Manifestation

Always remember. There is potential in you. All your virtues and power are waiting for you to manifest and use to fulfill your existence. No matter where you are, who you think you are and the circumstances you are in; you have all the right to accomplish your goals. Every single human being is worth every ounce of success the world has to offer.

When you start to implement all the goodness this book has to offer, all your fears and insecurities will begin to disappear. What replaces them are courage and knowledge. They are your sidekicks to go through that wonderful journey with you.

All you need to do is start with that very first step. Every journey starts with the visualization of your dream. From there, you need to grab on to your faith and belief. Slowly but surely, they will help carve the path to your success.

Here's to your powerful success!

Inner Strenght Manifesto

What 95% Of The People Do Not Know About Personal
Growth

Any individuals who are in the business of leading,
motivating and inspiring others should give careful
consideration to embarking on a self-development
program of any kind first to have a critical look at
them. This is important to knowing yourself well in
order to determine what areas that need further
improvement.

Once an area of improvement is identified, then fixing
it would be much simpler. I like to call this process the
"scientific way" because it is an empirical approach in
diagnosing the issues and rectifying it.
There is 3 processes involved in this:

- Identifying
- Admitting
- Addressing

We begin by first identifying our focus and gaps. If we
intend to change for the better, it is important we be
outright honest with ourselves by asking simple
questions first. What are our strengths, weaknesses
and aspirations? Write it down onto a piece of paper.

For example,

	Strengths	Weakness	Aspirations
A	Ambitious, disciplined, Goal-oriented	Lack of gratitude, selfish, overpromises, calculative	To be more kind, patient, and tolerant. To think ahead before committing
B	Meticulous, loving and caring, generous	Socially awkward, avoidance, stubbornness	To build more courage and confidence. To speak out, to be heard and dare to confront the matter

By these two individuals' examples, you can tell that they each have very distinct personalities. Since we are all brought up differently due to our teachings and environment, we are moulded to who we are today.

Some might argue certain characteristics (strengths and weaknesses) are passed down from generation to generation, but these can be tweaked, granted if you have the intention to change in the first place.

Strength – is the fundamental aspect of yourself. It is what makes you who you are today! Certain people are attracted to you because you exhibit these types of traits that they want to emulate or know you better.

Weakness – the other brother of strength and everyone has it whether they admit it or not. These are the traits you want to consider improving.

Aspirations – Usually associated with your hopes and ambitions in achieving something.

Back to the individuals' examples, Individual A is someone who is driven and ambitious and usually they are the people who are involved in corporate and sales line (I guess you can begin to picture some of your surrounding friends). They are dead right focused, goal- oriented and most likely loves challenges. On the flip side, they might turn out to be rather unkind and does not seem to appreciate the goodness in other people.

Now take a look at what you had wrote in the paper, I want you to embrace your strengths and begin to genuinely accept and acknowledge your weaknesses. Because you see, if you can't even accept that part of yours, it is very hard to move forward to the next stage.

The irony?

Most people write down their "weaknesses" and frown, either they think it is a small matter or they find it difficult to admit.
The truth is, this is what will actually happen:

It is not difficult to admit your weaknesses
By writing down your weaknesses, you not only learn to accept them but you have the conscious effort to do something about it

Before we delve into aspirations, I want you to begin by seeking honest opinions and feedback from the people whom you trust. This is an important exercise because earlier what you just did was "how you see yourself in the mirror".

The second exercise is about how other people look at you. Ask these questions to your close acquaintances, siblings or even your significant other!
If the feedback you get correlates with what you wrote down, then great! This makes it easier for you to improve on your weaknesses.

If it is different from what you have listed down, then you should compare the qualities that you have wrote down with that of the people around you. Go through them one by one and see which ones are relevant and which ones are not.

Here comes the third step, addressing. Addressing is all about taking actions. For example, take individual B, he listed down avoidance as his weak trait and has acknowledged it.

Therefore, he is addressing his weaknesses by taking necessary steps to meet his aspirations.

Most of us find this step as one of the toughest things to do. Why?

Because we have been "living" with our weaknesses for so long it has become a part of us. Maybe we are afraid that by discarding our trait, we lose a unique personality of ourselves?

Therefore, you need to think of your aspirations. Aspirations is what you intend to be but is still in the "work in progress" stage. You want to improve to be a better person and work on your weaknesses. However, your aspirations are meaningless unless you address it and take necessary actions.

Change can only begin by taking action and to be precise, MASSIVE ACTION. If you want something, you have to work for it; nothing comes free in this world. Heard of the saying, "No Pain, No Gain"?

Another mentality that most of us like to adopt is, "I will try my best". Well, trying is just not good enough, because in the end, if things do not work out well on our end, we will console ourselves by saying "at least I have tried."
Instead if you do seriously want to address your weaknesses and aspire to be who you set out to be, change your mind set by adopting a mentality that you will do anything it takes to be who you want to be. You need to remind yourself, you are changing for the better,

"NO MATTER WHAT"

In fact, treat this as your "mantra" moving forward. I have seen too many people giving up without putting up a good fight in life. They throw down the towel too quickly and not committed to change because they lack the determination and persistence.

Little Known Way To: Self Assurance!

For the purpose of the exercise, since individual B has exhibited socially awkward symptoms and do have the aspirations to be more courageous and confident, I will continue to use him for the remainder of this book.

Not everyone is born confident, in fact, confidence is built throughout time. Some children are blessed to have brought up in an environment where discussion is free within the family. Hence, they are able to debate and give their thoughts and views. That will ultimately shape and contribute to the person they are today.

That is not to say that children who are brought up in a strict family environment will end up having lack of confidence. No doubt that this will more or less impede their personal development in the adult stage, however, it is not the end of the world.
Thankfully, I have found some certain quick methods that work like a charm!

- Phasing out certain voices
- Following your heart
- Morale support
- "You can do it too!"

The first step to improving your confidence is phasing out that internal voice in your mind that keeps telling you it is not possible; begin to block it out and ask yourself "what is the worst-case scenario?" After experiencing something you feared doing for the first time, you realize that it was not as frightening as you thought it would be.

Have you ever experienced the situation when you lack of the courage or the confidence to approach your crush? That is because you have constantly built an obstacle as high as the mountain it becomes a daunting task. Follow your heart, you have allowed your brain to determine your logical and reality of your life but how can you truly live your life if you have not tried it yet? Are you afraid of embarrassment or people making fun of you?

Thus, my question to you is "so what?", if you have not tried it, how will you know the outcome? Besides, guess what? No one will actually remember that blooper few years down the road. Better to live life with no regrets than looking back later in life thinking "what if?"

Moral support is also the key to beefing up your confidence level, always confide in someone that you can trust and help you feel better about yourself. Opening up about your fears and inner feelings will not only make you feel better but also it will give you another perspective of how other people see you. Besides, listening to someone who tells you can do something WILL give you the extra push into making it happen.

Always consider the fact in your mind that if it can be done by others, you can do it too! For example, I truly respect and admire individuals such as Lizzie Velasquez &Nick Vujicic because they are the people born with unfortunate circumstances and yet they do not allow their shortcoming to get a hold of them, instead they carry themselves confidently.

Now that I have disclosed the quick methods to you, the next step is simple, it only requires you to make the FIRST move, and the rest will just follow. Quoting Lao Tzu, "A journey of a thousand miles begins with a single step."

How quickly you can see a change within yourself is really dependent on your determination and persistence. It is all depended on how badly you want to change as well as adopting the "no matter what" mentality.

How Positivity Enables You To Achieve More in Life

You may notice that some people who have already possessed almost everything they desire in their lives are still not happy. Why? This may be due to the fact that everything they have ever worked for is only to obtain the approval and recognition of others. When they face disapproval and disagreement from others, they are easily affected by it. They seek for external validation.

Be it with your family members and workplace, we are bound to have interactions almost every day in our lives. Whether we like it or not with interactions, comes with expectations and approvals.

For instance, if we are trying so hard to get our bosses approval or recognition for our job performance. When we do not get the approval, this is when we will feel disappointed where it may affect our self-esteem.

One way of resolving this matter is by confronting your boss and understand where he/she deems you short... (Still short of the confidence booster? Please refer back above before attempting this)

For example, after the whole discussion, it turns out that he is unsatisfied with you in areas such as:

Your boss' view	Your reasons
Not being a team player	I have completed my work tasks, do I have to do my other colleagues work?
Not participating in company's event after working hours	I want to spend quality time with my wife/husband and children
Not amicable enough	I was not brought up to be a social butterfly

Notice the "complaints" and "issues" your boss has? He/she is actually pointing out on your personal character rather than your work delivery... After all, how dare he/she? This is a personal attack to your personality!

There are several outcomes after the discussion:

You truly believe your boss has pointed out your weaknesses and you deem it is time to change
You do not believe what he said is true, but because you respect your boss, it pains you that you are not able to get his recognition or "approval"

You do not believe what he/she said is true, but you are "playing along" with it
You do not care what your boss says, and frankly, since he/she has so many issues with you, it is just about the time for you to begin looking for the next job
If you pick option A, congratulations! That means you are open to criticism and thus, able to make the change. (Remember, Admittance?)

Unfortunately, most people fall either into option B or D. Not many people believe they have flaws themselves and it is even more difficult to accept it if it had been told by the higher-ups (e.g. parents, bosses, authority figures).

Honestly, picking Option B is not a healthy solution because you are just acting how your boss wants you to behave. Let's face it, that is not your true personal character and the reason you are doing it? What else, if it is not for your monthly salary? Figuratively speaking, this solution is like using a band-aid on a bullet hole. Painting the picture clearly here, what will happen in the next several months, since you are tolerating your boss and genuinely do not accept what he says to be exactly the truth is you will start to enter into a negative phase.

Because the chemistry was wrong to begin with, you will end up being miserable and unhappy every single day! Waking up daily is like a torture, there is nothing to look forward to in life, I guess now you are considering Option D? After all, there is this saying, "If I do not work for you, I am pretty sure there are plenty of job opportunities out there for my selection!"

Guess what? What if the next job opportunity you end up with even a worse boss? (You can argue that you might get a more "understanding" boss, but realistically speaking, you are just escaping the issue at hand).

This is where the positive mindset adoption is crucial, and there are two ways that we can achieve this: Treating all of these as "noises" or "phases" in your life Do not allow yourself to fall into despair (Digging the hole deeper than it already is).

Have you reached a stage where you just find your life mundane and unproductive? Where every day is just grinding the mill? There is nothing exciting to look forward to?

If that's the case, may I suggest you start evaluating your life by giving it a sense of purpose. Most people when they have hit the middle age of 30, have lost their sense of purpose and their drive to pursue their dreams.

This can be due to the fact that they are busy chasing their careers and have lost their identity as well as aspirations in becoming who they truly are.
They no longer dare to take excessive risks, fear of losing their jobs, and prioritising security in life. Hence, after working 10 – 20 years all in the name of family, they began to lose their initial ambition when they were young.

Without purpose, what happened is they start to mind

all the smallest unpleasant details in their daily lives, workplace or family interaction. Small little annoyance can be amplified to a huge magnitude such as receiving a minor criticism from your colleagues, getting an argument with other motor vehicles and other irrelevant matters.

So, begin by identifying your raison d'être1, because by having that firmly planted in your mind, you will begin "phasing" out these issues or treating as "noises", because after all, these are all small issues that do not matter if you possess an ultimate goal in mind. Allow me to elaborate further, let's take a simple example, if your goal is to be the top chef in the cooking industry, you will not let any other people tell you otherwise; that they tell you have no talent or you are unqualified, even your parents frown upon your dreams just because they want you to be who they want you to be.

Explaining to them is fruitless, especially if they are so fixated for you to become a lawyer/doctor/engineer for instance. If they can understand, great! Unfortunately, I reckon not all parents understand.

It is not about influencing others first. This is more about enduring and making some small sacrifices so

you can achieve your final goal. Sometimes, giving in or losing a battle here and there, allows you to win the war and that is what matters the most!
What about my feelings?

What about the things that I stand for? Don't I have a say in what I want?

What I learn in life and what I am about to tell you is this. If you are capable and have the power to do so, just DO it! If not, there is no point of you "complaining" these issues because at the end of the day it gets you nowhere. So, should you be admitting defeat and accept the outcome? No! Begin by strategizing and planning on how to achieve your goals against the odds. That my readers, is a much better way to channel your energy rather than complaining!

The next point, will you allow yourself to fall into despair when the whole world goes against you? You just want to do your "job" and to be left alone, but it just still feels like everything you do has gone wrong, that somehow you are blaming god for all the misfortunes that has happened to you... You even question, "Why me?"

If you allow your unconsciousness to dictate your life,

inadvertently you are feeding into the negative aspects. There are constantly two sides fighting inside you. The positive and the negative, ultimately one will prevail. So, which will win? – The one you choose to feed... So, every time you feel despair, make it a conscious effort you refuse to fall into the dark side. That you are much better than this! Some people even consider chanting a mantra to remind themselves that.

How To Be A Rockstar And Attract People Effortlessly

You could literally be a Rockstar (or something close to that) and influence others to act the way you want via powerful communication techniques.
How do rock stars amass a huge loyal crowd that follows them?

Is it due to their...

- Energy? Vigour? Vibes?

- Personality? Character? Portrayal?

- Fame? Prominence?

- Message? Communication?

First, you will have more energy within you. By now, you have adopted the "no matter what" and "can do" attitude. This is the type of energy people around you will take notice.

In fact, initially they might even be uncomfortable seeing the changes in you, but that is a good thing! Would you rather be with a friend who keeps telling you "it is impossible" or "it can't be done"? These types of friends emit a HUGE negative energy or vibe. Look at a Rock star, do they have that?

When you carry yourself with assurance, just like a rockstar, people will begin to listen to what you have to say (which they did not last time). It is more so, when you make a stand for something you truly believe in and what you say resonates with what they think. Always remember that you can be your own rockstar, in fact all of these will unconsciously be released out by you! Trust me, when you have truly attained the desired confidence level and established the positive mind-set, there is so much more that you can achieve in life!

Manifestation At Its' Core

Manifestation is simple to understand and yet it is easy to incorporate together with what you just read above! By understanding and practicing manifestation, you will be able to explicitly double the abundance's life! Let's take it further to the next level by understanding the general concept of manifestation.

- Start appreciating your life
- Free yourself from desires
- Turning your desires into goals

This is a very important concept which can take some time to absorb, but first off, you need to admire your life. You need to believe in the concept that everything which you have in your life now is because of your own CHOICE.

Stop blaming third parties for your loss and failures and begin to accept the fact you are responsible and accountable for your own life.

Most people do not appreciate the small little things they have in life because they take it for granted. For example, respect and love your dear parents because there are those out there who have lost their parents. Although you might be struggling in life, be fortunate you are still able to pay your rent and put food on the table.

When you desire something, you inadvertently declare that you do not have something. These two are much closely related than you think they are. It is fine having desires. After all, it is what gives you "purpose" and drives you to work towards the goal. All you need to do is to always desire something within your grasp and according to your means.

And ... translate that desire into goals! To put it into context, manifesting you are in line for promotion is much easier than becoming the next Warren Buffett. With the promotion goal in mind, you'll get to know the next thing to get towards the promotion you desired.

The more you think about it, the nearer you will be in completing the tasks at hand. Soon, it will become second nature to you.

2 Simple Ways To Practice Manifestation

If you are a devout practitioner of manifestation, then you will know how useful and beneficial manifestation is. Here are 2 simple ways to practice manifestation; Setting up the goal

Visualization and attaching positive emotions with

your goals

Begin the first step by setting up a goal (in some circumstance, "purpose") in life. This is rather obvious and easy to understand, but if you intend to embark on practicing manifestation, then your goals need to be more specific and personal in nature. Examples are, losing weight, quit smoking or even going back to school.

All this might seem menial or even hilarious in the beginning, but once you get hold of things, there is this power in the universe which will make your subconscious mind to act on the instructions to manifest them.

Now that you have the goal in mind, just sitting at home and thinking about it will not bring you any closer to the goal that you want. Instead, you need to make a definite and exact plan which you can follow. Most people think manifestation is some kind of magic and everything will come true just by the degree of "how hard I wish", but the reality is, thinking is just one part of manifestation and there is more to work with.

Some goals are realistic and achievable, some are not.

The beauty of manifestation is once you begin thinking about that goal, your subconscious mind will guide you through the specific and exact way.

Begin this exercise by writing the easier things you want and the steps which are needed to be completed. Then, move on to the bigger goals.

Besides that, you need to create a platform where the process contributing to the goal can be monitored. This will enable you to monitor and address any issues that need attention or redesigning. Never forget the enthusiast you who chose such a goal in the first place.

Simply because once you lose the initial excitement and momentum, it will further jeopardize your achievement.

Therefore, it is very important to set smaller and less demanding goals that will help to create the confidence level to encourage you to aim for bigger goals at the next juncture.

For this to truly achieve, you must discipline yourself to achieve it.

Revisit this exercise as often as you can because at

times you might even find better ways to improve on the steps that you had initially thought.

Once you are accustomed to it, ironically, you will take this as a fun exercise and begin to enjoy the process.

What you need to do now is to write down your goals.

At the same time, jot down all the possible methods to achieve it. It doesn't need to be accurate just yet. The purpose is to keep pushing you towards the reality of achieving that goal.

For example, you are projecting yourself having a wonderful significant other, owning a beautiful home, travel anywhere you want and getting excited about it!

By using imagery as a motivating tool, you will be able to "see and feel" the outcome. This helps keep the excitement and momentum going to help you move forward.

It might be tough at first, and there is no guarantee that the manifestation will directly change your reality (at least, initially), but one thing is for sure that it will affect your life by influencing your subconscious.

Hence, this will lead to a better mindset, more focused and happier YOU!